FUEL FOR THE BURNING HEART

A Daily Devotional

FUEL FOR THE BURNING HEART
A Daily Devotional

DAVID FRITCH – TANNON HERMAN

CRISTINA HERMAN – COURTNEY YATES

CODY MYERS – MICHELLE SMITH

JOSHUA SWARNY – COLTON McHONE

For more information:
Burning Ones Mission Base
230 North Broadway Ave
Shawnee, OK 74801
www.burningones.com
405.225.7909

Dedication

We would like to dedicate this book to all the Burning Ones that we have had the privilege of coming through our doors. May the flames of your lives continue to ignite a passion for Jesus in those around you.

And also to David Fritch. As you read this book, may you be reminded of the worth of your sacrifices and the enduring promises of God for your life. Thank you for dreaming big!

Acknowledgements

We would like to thank Dr. Linda Fritch and the Burning Ones Staff for so graciously laboring in their editing so that this book might be published in an extraordinarily brief amount of time.

We would like to thank all the Leadership Development students who provided the material for this book. Your contributions and patience are priceless, and we look forward to reading the next book you write or album you record.

We would like to thank Tannon Herman for dreaming up this idea; David Fritch for inspiring a community of writers; and, Cristina Herman for never failing to provide the support and encouragement needed to complete a project like this.

We would like to thank Colton McHone for designing the cover of our very first publication. Your creativity will never be forgotten or without appreciation.

Lastly, we would like to acknowledge the lover of our souls, Jesus. These pages are filled with encounters with Your beauty, majesty, kindness, fierceness and love. Your story will always be our inspiration!

Endorsements

"God is raising up a new wave of revivalist and apostolic messengers in the earth. These are the men and women that are fueled by the Presence of God and burn with desire that His name would be great among the nations (Mal. 1:11)! David Fritch is equipping, training, and releasing these ministers through the Burning Ones Internship. The heartbeat of the internship beats with the very heartbeat of God for this generation. David and the Burning Ones team have worked hand in hand with our ministry, and we can fully endorse, promote, and cheer on the awesome work that God is doing in their midst. So go ahead! Believe God for a season of radical transformation and growth and be a part of the Burning Ones Internship! Your life will never be the same!"

Jeff Struss Jr.
Director of Lynchburg House of Prayer
Lynchburg, VA

"The Burning Ones Internship is one of the most powerful, anointed and effective training schools that we have in the BURN 24-7 Global Movement. David Fritch is a phenomenally gifted teacher, mentor and leader who is raising up a generation of revivalists who will mark a generation with the fire of God."

Sean Feucht
Founder of Burn 24-7
Harrisburg, PA

"Burning Ones are amazing! We love these guys! Whenever they come to us to minister in our city they are servants and have such joyful, thankful hearts. They just want to worship Jesus and bless others! They are just as comfortable with Christians and non-Christians alike. They are a breath of fresh air to our ministry! We love them and feel like we should host them anytime that they want to come - they are such a blessing to us!"

Richard Thompson
Director, YWAM Las Vegas
Las Vegas, NV

"David Fritch and the Burning Ones Internship are highly recommended. David is a stellar fiery man of God with a pure heart, loves people, and is giving his all to the next generation. I recommend him as a person and any ministry that he is leading. I would send my own children to the Burning Ones Discipleship School and there is no higher recommendation that I can give."

Keith Luker
Freewind Ministries & Prophetic Worship Radio
Martinez, CA

"The Burning Ones Internship truly lives up to its name! If you are looking for a place to get discipled into your calling as a burning man or woman look no further! The Burning Ones is not only a training school but a fully immersed lifestyle of revival! Get set on fire in radical love and the world will come watch you burn!"

Jeremy Bardwell
Director of Fire & Fragrance Harrisburg
Harrisburg, PA

"David Fritch and the Burning Ones are a pioneering ministry that is forming true disciples of Jesus Christ with a depth of devotion and empowerment that smacks of early New Testament Christianity. As a long time friend and partner in the gospel, I have found few men with such a high measure of the humility, integrity and zeal that is on full display in David's life."

Adam Cates
Big House Church
Chesapeake, VA

Table of Contents

Foreword

The entire Burn 24-7 global grassroots movement was birthed on the foundation of a zealous and fiery first-love for the presence of God. We were just a bunch of hungry and wild college kids holed up in a stuffy dorm room longing for more than religious rhetoric and shallow-watered Christianity. From the revelation of our own personal apathy and lack, we desperately cried out for a greater glimpse, depth and encounter. He answered us by igniting a fire in our hearts that would last through the watches of the night and eventually spread to the nations of the world and back again.

Seven years and hundreds of furnaces, trainings, schools, initiatives and breakthroughs later, we are ever still dependent on sustaining those precious moments like what ignited this global blaze. In the midst of increasing growth, expansion, maturation and mounting pressure, we must daily and intentionally "repent and return to those things we did at first" (Rev 2:5). Without this marked reality in our lives, families and communities, we are just a network full of musicians, nomads and misfits that boast nothing but a cool flame logo reminding us of what once used to be. But with this first-love flame alive and active in our hearts, we possess HIM and that is all we need!

The pages you are about to read were penned by a ragtag crew of young zealous, fiery burners that still remain at the heart and soul of our movement today. They are raw, unpolished and heart-on-your-sleeve devotionals that will inspire and encourage you in stewarding the fire to "never go out" on the altar of your heart. These words, stories and testimonies are dripping with first-love revelation and give language for a generation to an entire generation on this same quest. Read, meditate and pray and your heart, too, shall begin to burn.

Sean Feucht
Founder and Director, Burn 24-7

Intimacy with God

This is a presence-centered lifestyle where everything the believer is and does is founded in an intimate relationship with God. Communion with God is based on the revelation of His unconditional love and passionate pursuit of man. This develops a culture of dependency on God, a life flowing from rest, and a security that we are loved in our weakness. We see intimacy with God as our highest pursuit and pleasure.

—Core Value #1—

THE ONE THING

BY: CRISTINA HERMAN

> "One thing I ask from the Lord, this only do I seek: that I may dwell in the house of the Lord all the days of my life, to gaze on the beauty of the Lord and to seek Him in His temple."
>
> Psalms 27:4

It was June 2008, the summer after I graduated college. I was in Matamoros, Mexico on a mission trip only weeks away from moving to Puerto Rico to pursue what I thought was my dream, to become a physician. As I was sitting in a worship and prayer set at 8 am, listening to a passionate worshiper pouring out his heart to the Lord, I was reading Psalm 27:4. Tears streamed down my face, as I realized I too wanted to lay everything down to know the Lord. David's words, "one thing I ask" came off the page of the Bible and entered into my heart. This was my deepest desire and surpassed every other dream, passion and aspiration. Did I really want to be a doctor or was that just what I thought I had to be?

I was at a crossroads. I had to make a decision. Would I go after everything I spent my life preparing for, or would I follow this deep desire to know Him more? The cry of my heart was to truly behold Him. It was worth everything to me. It was the hardest decision of my life, but the best one I made. It was worth laying everything down to take time to pursue Jesus, to really know Him. He is truly worth everything. To know Him is my highest pleasure and one pursuit. It cost me everything - money, relationships, and career opportunities - but I gained everything, Him! He is my prize; He is my great reward.

"We see intimacy with God as our highest pursuit and pleasure."

God is looking for a generation that will lay everything down to pursue this one thing: to know Him. It is from this place that real purpose, identity and life flows out - the place of communion with Him. As I pursued Him, He began to heal my heart and really fill the voids in my life. This is what I was made for: to love Him and be loved by Him. His love came in and began to transform me simply by being with Him in His presence.

Raise up a generation with one heart's cry,
To know you, God, and be known by You![1]

APPLICATION

What have you had to sacrifice in order to pursue the Lord? Is there something else God is asking you to lay down?

_____

_____

_____

_____

_____

_____

_____

_____

_____

ACTIVATION

Take time to dialogue with the Lord about what it means for God to be your highest pleasure and pursuit. What does this look like in your life?

_____

_____

_____

_____

_____

_____

_____

_____

_____

_____

_____

_____

_____

---

[1] Lyrics taken from a song written by Cristina Herman.

RESTING INTO INTIMACY

BY: MICHELLE SMITH

"My soul finds rest in God alone; my salvation comes from Him."

Psalm 62:1

Is it possible that we can be led into intimacy with God through resting in His presence? Often our souls become so busy that we lose touch with God. Even in well-doing, we find ourselves striving to simply be with God. There are deep places in our hearts that God is longing to touch. He desires intimacy with us, and He desires that we live a lifestyle of rest. King David illustrates this perfectly in Psalm 62:1: "My soul finds rest in God *alone*." He wants our hearts; He wants our rest.

In 2011, I spent the summer living in Jerusalem. I arrived in early June after finishing a rigorous semester in college and working full-time. While I was there, my only expectation (except for a few minor chores at the house) was to worship God. I was eager to get into the presence of God and recognized that this summer was a season for just me and God.

What I didn't expect was to have to fight through one of the most uncomfortable transitions I have ever experienced. As soon as I arrived, I joyfully spent two full days in the prayer room. By day three, however, I was absolutely restless. I filled my days exploring the city, being in the prayer room, reading, writing, and doing anything I could to keep myself busy. I thought I was searching for purpose, but really, I was searching for something to "do". I had never been in a place where I was not expected to actually "do" anything.

"This develops... a life flowing from rest."

Shifting from one of the busiest semesters of my life into a schedule free from obligations was far more challenging than I could have ever anticipated. I learned that I didn't know how to rest. I didn't know how to slow down and simply "be". God was calling me into a place of deep intimacy with Him, but first, He needed to teach me how to rest.

Slowly but surely, I felt less of an obligation to constantly be "doing" things in His presence, and began entering into rest.

I spent many hours sitting on my bed meditating on the Lord. In that simple and beautiful place, God began to unlock a deeper experience of intimacy with Him. When I look back at my "Summer with God", as I call it, my favorite memories were when I was alone in my bedroom meditating on the Lord, experiencing His extravagant love pouring over me.

APPLICATION

What is keeping you from entering into the Lord's rest? Why?

_____

_____

_____

_____

_____

_____

_____

_____

_____

_____

_____

ACTIVATION

Spend some time with the Lord simply meditating on Him (don't read, write, paint, play music, or do anything). Ask the Holy Spirit to teach you how to rest as a lifestyle.

BE MY DISTRACTION

BY: COLTON MCHONE

"Why are you cast down, O my soul, and why are you disquieted within me? Hope in God; for I shall again praise him, my help and my God."

Psalm 43:5, NKJV

It's scary sometimes to see what's in your heart, but it's so worth it. I sat bored in my office at home and, honestly, trying to get anywhere away from God so that I wouldn't have to see my heart up-close. I had gone through some deliverance the night before, and I knew there was more to come but was scared to find out what it was. I was doing everything I could to avoid talking to God about what was going on in my newly-healed heart. I sat there for a while making a list of things I could do rather than confront my heart.

Finally, God, in that sweet fatherly whisper, said to me, "Be still." I looked up and said, "Okay." In that moment I felt so loved and peaceful. I then sat down and began to journal with God about everything that was on my mind and all the things that I was scared to say out loud. As I was writing, He began speaking things into me that He wanted me to know about myself. It was truths about who I am; truths I needed to hear which invited me into more healing. As I sat there with music playing in the background, and the presence of God so real in the room, I realized that He really is kind and gentle. I wasn't scared anymore.

"Communion with God is based on the revelation of His unconditional love and passionate pursuit of man."

I was able to empty out everything in my heart in that moment and come into His freedom. The power of His kind and gentle words led me to wholeness. The presence of God brought me unspeakable joy and a pure heart. Now, my heart is burning to know how He wants to build and mold me into a son and more fervent lover of Jesus. I'm so glad that God didn't let me hide and that I said "yes" to His call. I'm so glad that He saved me from myself.

This is what He wants for you. This is the dream of His heart.
You are the dream of His heart!

APPLICATION

*Why do you think we sometimes run from God when He's dealing with
matters of the heart?*

---

*What do you think it would look like if we let God in every time he knocked
on the door of our hearts?*

ACTIVATION

*Write down some of the things that you've been scared to talk to God about.
Once finished, try to start a conversation with the Lord about what you've
written down.*

A Friend In Need Is A Friend Indeed
by: Cody Myers

"Blessed are the poor in spirit, for theirs is the kingdom of Heaven."

Matthew 5:3

The term *dependent* can sometimes have a negative connotation. In this case, however, it is one of the best revelations I can receive as a child of God. Why is it so difficult for me to truly believe that I absolutely, completely and undoubtedly need God every moment of every day? I think we avoid total dependency because we've been taught by society, peers, or even our families that being needy is bad. Here's a little secret: we are all needy! God designed us with a burning need for Him.

At the beginning of the Burning Ones 2012 semester, we discussed Matthew 5:1 extensively. I had always thought being poor in spirit meant being content with what you have because God is your portion. I discovered it means to have an aching longing for God to permeate every area of your life because He is the only reason for living. After grasping a small fragment of this new revelation, I wanted to be desperate for Him. I wanted my relationship with Him to be based on utmost need, as well as desire. I wanted to cultivate this mindset for the rest of my life because I never wanted to think I could survive without Him.

To be poor in spirit is to recognize that nothing and no one can fulfill me other than the Holy Presence of Abba Father. My spirit is incomplete when lacking constant communion with God's Spirit. He created me with the intention of being my closest, most intimate friend, and He loves to be the source of everything that pertains to my life. A lot of Christians think they stop needing God after they accept salvation from sin. The truth is, He is salvation! Jesus is the answer to our highest needs and greatest desires.

"...a culture of dependency on God..."

It's a daily choice to be poor in spirit. I have to decide uncompromisingly that He's my only plan, the only One who can satisfy me. I have to train my appetite to desire the very best, and develop a hunger so deep and so ravenous that temporary satisfactions are not enough. If I want the Kingdom, I can have it, but how much do I want?

When I am fully dependent on God alone, I receive all He wants to give. It's rather ironic, really. If I stay poor in spirit, I have it all. The key is to remember that "nothing I do can earn what He wants to lavish on me." My Father's greatest longing is to share Himself with me. He has adopted me into the Royal Family, meaning I am heir to the very foundations of the world – whoa! The "poor in spirit" mindset isn't an excuse to act like a slave in my relationship with God; it's to keep me in a place to receive His very heart!

ACTIVATION

How do you feel about the concept of being poor in spirit? Are you willing to be totally dependent on God? Why or why not?

_____

_____

_____

_____

_____

_____

APPLICATION

Meditate/journal on the Beatitudes (Matthew 5). Ask Holy Spirit to show you why dependency is an important part of intimacy.

_____

_____

_____

_____

_____

_____

_____

_____

_____

_____

_____

_____

LEAD ME INTO THE WILDERNESS
BY: COURTNEY YATES

"Therefore I am now going to allure her; I will lead her into the desert and speak tenderly to her. There I will give her back her vineyards, and will make the Valley of Achor (trouble) a door of hope. There she will sing as in the days of her youth, as in the day she came up out of Egypt. In that day, declares the Lord, you will call me 'my husband'; you will no longer call me 'my master.'"

Hosea 2: 14-16

The fifth day of the Burning Ones Discipleship School was a day I will never forget. One of our leaders, Tannon Herman, led worship that morning and the Word of the Lord came upon him saying, "I am so jealous for your love! I furiously fight against the ones you give your love and attention to, which is only intended for Me. I want all of you." God is furious for all of our love and devotion and He was letting us know.

Whenever I thought about God's furious love for us, I always imagined He was looking at me with anger because of how I would turn to "other lovers" instead of Him. That morning He revealed to me a new perspective about His furious love for me. He showed me how He looks at the enemy, the "other lovers", with anger and judgment and looks upon us, His bride, with a fiery, yet gentle, passion in His eyes. The Father looks at us and sees His perfect creation that He is proud of and longs to be in relationship with. It is true that He is a jealous God. He judges those things that turn our hearts and gaze from Him. That was the beginning of what I like to call, a Hosea season, for me.

"Communion with God is based on the revelation of His unconditional love and passionate pursuit of man."

During that season, I was on a journey with the Lord, where He stripped all of my comforts away so that I could see that He is my husband. He is my first love, my solid foundation. I had placed other things and people in my heart and life in the place where He was supposed to be. It was time for Him to lead me into the desert and restore our relationship the way He intended it to be.

The Lord healed my heart and my mind as He spoke tenderly to me about whom I am and His love for me.

APPLICATION

How does reading this message of God's furious love for you make you feel? Why?

_____

_____

_____

_____

_____

In which way do you see yourself in your relationship with the Lord; as his servant or as His bride? Why?

_____

_____

_____

_____

_____

_____

ACTIVATION

Take some time to reflect on this message with the Lord. Ask the Holy Spirit if there are any "other lovers" that He wants you to let go of.

_____

_____

_____

_____

_____

_____

_____

_____

_____

_____

_____

_____

LOVE IS MY REWARD

BY: TANNON HERMAN

"Sixty queens there may be, and eighty concubines, and virgins beyond number; but my dove, my perfect one, is unique... the [virgins] saw her and called her blessed; the queens and concubines praised her."

Song of Solomon 6:8-9

When I was a teenager something very strange happened in my relationship with Jesus. I had been faithfully running after Him, pursuing greater knowledge of His love, but then He responded with a somewhat confusing message: "Tannon, if it helps, try to love me like you would love another person. How would you show another person that you love them?" What? I recall sitting in my room wondering, "Okay, is this really the Lord? Have I completely lost my mind?" As I continued my conversation with Him, He began to reveal His jealousy for my affections. I felt awkward listening to the Lord describe how He wanted me to relate with Him in this new season; however, it opened me up to a new experience of intimacy with Him. My attitude towards Jesus changed as a result of His invitation, and I felt liberated to really love Him.

"... where everything the believer is and does is founded in an intimate relationship with God."

In that season I began to write songs, poems and letters to Jesus. It wasn't as difficult as the times previously because I no longer cared about who read or heard these creative conversations. My relationship with Jesus became deeply personal and expressive. I learned how to have a two-way relationship with Jesus. My excitement grew as I continued to anticipate dialogue with Him, and it became normal for Him to actually respond to me.

What happened to me in that conversation with the Lord was an invitation for a new experience in intimacy with Jesus. He was calling me into a deeper level of knowing Him. Since that challenge was issued to me to love Him deeply, I have accepted many more invitations in my relationship with the Lord. In Solomon's passage, he describes different experiences of intimacy: the virgin, the concubine, the queen, and the dove. Each of these identities enjoys different levels of intimacy and authority, but only the dove possesses the fullness of both. Love and power is the dove's prize of the intimacy with God. In this place of "unique" covenant, we are empowered to love and be loved. As doves we are entrusted with divine authority to partner with our Bridegroom in establishing His kingdom on the earth. We are called to oneness with God in such a way. This is your invitation. He is your reward.

APPLICATION

What is keeping you from going deeper in your intimacy with the Lord?

_____

_____

_____

_____

ACTIVATION

Begin writing a love letter to the Lord. Write down anything and everything, even if it feels strange to you. Next, ask the Lord to respond and allow Him to write you a love letter in your journal.

_____

_____

_____

_____

_____

_____

_____

_____

_____

_____

_____

_____

_____

_____

_____

_____

BEAUTY IN BROKENNESS
BY: CRISTINA HERMAN

> "You are altogether beautiful, my darling; there is no flaw in you."
>
> Song of Songs 4:7

I believe that one of the greatest longings of the human heart is to be fully known and loved in our weakness. It is this longing that is only truly fulfilled in relationship with God. He knows everything about us and yet chooses to love us anyway.

His love gives us security - a security that no matter what we do, His love for us will never change. It is a love not based on performance, failure or success, but a love that simply is because He is Love.

My experience of love always seemed to be based on my behavior or performance. To think that there is a love not tied to *any* expectations, which cannot be taken away or earned, went against what I knew in my life to be true. It has been a journey of discovering a love that is beyond my understanding. The more I experience God, the more I understand His love really is constant and unchanging and is not afraid in the midst of my weakness or failure. Understanding His love that knows no bounds has been foundational to my own healing and transformation.

This verse from Song of Songs has been an anchor of truth in my life. When the Father looks

"This develops... a security that we are loved in our weakness."

at me, it is like He sees His Son – perfectly beautiful and without flaw. There is nothing I can do to be separated from His love. What I see as weakness and flaw, He perceives as lovely and from that place calls me into the real me. He calls me beautiful at my weakest, darkest, and most horrible moments. He loves and accepts me in my most vulnerable states, even when I feel ugly or scared. When Jesus saw me from the cross, He said "*You*, child, are worth it all! *You*, child, are beautiful, even now, in your sin. *You* are worthy of Love. This is not who you are. I see the real you. I'm doing this so you can become the real you that I see!" I am beginning to really believe this.

I am loved in my weakness I'm dark but I am lovely
I am loved in my sin, you never give up on me[2]

APPLICATION

How do you normally respond when you fail? Why?

_____

_____

_____

_____

How does it make you feel to know that God loves you in your weakness?

_____

_____

_____

_____

_____

ACTIVATION

Take some time to ask God to reveal any lies you've believed about His love. Repent and fall out of agreement with those lies, and ask God to give you truths about His love for you.

_____

_____

_____

_____

_____

_____

_____

_____

_____

_____

_____

_____

[2] Lyrics from "Loved in Weakness" by Cristina Herman

TURN UP THE SILENCE
BY: DAVID FRITCH

"Be still and know that I am God"

Psalm 46:10a

Who would have ever thought that rest was so difficult? We gathered at the farm where our discipleship students were living in order to experiment with our first Sabbath day. We agreed to spend the morning in complete silence and to spend our time however the Spirit led us. I wandered off into the woods with excitement in my heart to encounter God in a new way but was soon overwhelmed by a surge of anxious thoughts.

I quickly realized I didn't know how to rest in the Lord, and that much of my walk with God was rooted in what I could say to Him, ask Him for or do for Him. After about an hour of wrestling with my thoughts I gave into the peace that was pursuing my heart. I spent the remainder of my time lying on a blanket under the most incredible oak tree, drinking deeply of the glory of creation. My heart swelled with the beauty of God and every second seemed to be so rich with the awareness of His presence. Time slipped away very quickly, and I was disappointed when my time of rest with the Lord was over.

I've rarely experienced the kind of peace I did that day. I was overwhelmed by Papa's love. It hit me that He didn't want anything from me. He didn't want my intercession, or even to give me any great revelation. He just wanted to be with me. For the rest of the day I walked in the sweetness of rest and found it easy to access His presence in every situation I encountered.

"A life flowing from rest..." He has called us to live a life to and from rest and it all begins with being still. When we enter into silence and rest we will find that He has been eager to meet with us.

APPLICATION

Why do you think it is hard for us to sit in silence and rest in the Lord?

_____

_____

_____

_____

What would your life look like if you lived it from a place of rest?

_____

_____

_____

_____

_____

What is the value of silent prayer?

_____

_____

_____

_____

_____

ACTIVATION

Take 1 hour this week to spend in silence and when you are done journal about your experience.

_____

_____

_____

_____

_____

_____

_____

_____

_____

_____

_____

_____

Covenant Community

A fellowship of believers unified by and committed to the pursuit of God and love for one another. This is a safe non-judgmental environment where one can be himself and cultivate vulnerability without the fear of being changed by someone. It is a community that lives in the light, overcomes struggles and fights for one another's dreams.

—Core Value #2—

COV-LOVE

BY: MICHELLE SMITH

"Be devoted to one another in brotherly love. Honor one another above yourselves."

Romans 12:10

The summer before I moved to Oklahoma, I had a dream that I was among a group of people of all different ages, ethnic groups, appearances, and giftings. We were in an upper room praying together. I knew that we were working together in unity for a single purpose of bringing the Kingdom of God to the earth. The strongest sense I had from this dream was that we were living together in the spirit of brotherly love.

In order for an entire community to live together in covenant, they must also live together in brotherly love. When I made the move to Shawnee, I was immediately embraced as if I had been part of the family forever. Not only had I found a kindred spirit among an entire group of people, but I had been effortlessly transplanted into a *community*. When I experienced the embrace of brotherly love, I was fully seen and known in all of my weakness and foolishness, and yet I was still fully loved. This experience of sincere brotherly love enabled me to embrace myself in a new way. I was finally free to be exactly who God created me to be - without shame or fear of rejection. Living in an environment that pursues covenant community through brotherly love has opened doors for me to experience the Father's perfect love for His family.

"A fellowship of believers unified by... love for one another."

This covenant community bears the evidence of the fruit of the spirit, the genuine hunger for the presence of God, and the value for each individual person who is a part of it. My literal and metaphorical dreams for community have become a reality as I have been embraced as a part of this family. Though my birth family is far away, I am among family here in Oklahoma.

APPLICATION

God created us for relationship and to be part of a family. In what ways have you experienced brotherly love? What has God revealed to you about brotherly love? How have you honored another before yourself?

_____

_____

_____

_____

_____

_____

_____

_____

_____

_____

_____

_____

_____

_____

ACTIVATION

Ask God to show you how you can demonstrate a greater measure of brotherly love to those around you. Ask the Holy Spirit to reveal to you someone who is in need of family. Reach out to him or her and welcome them into the family.

_____

_____

_____

_____

_____

_____

_____

_____

_____

_____

_____

LOVE KNOWS NO FEAR
BY: CODY MYERS

"There is no fear in love. But perfect love drives out fear, because fear has to do with punishment..."

1 John 4:18a

What is it that holds most of us back from achieving our dreams, sharing our hearts, trusting God, and being ourselves? It is the sneaky little liar named Fear. I have dealt with fear in more areas of my life than I can count. I was even scared to tell anyone I was afraid because I didn't know it was acceptable for Christians to have fears. How twisted was that? I was so busy trying to live an exemplary life for those around me that I didn't take the time to dig into my heart and find out if there was anything holding me back. I was afraid to be weak.

Being in the Burning Ones and experiencing covenant community was like a breath of fresh air. I was submerged in a culture that was working toward perfect love by making God's unconditional love the foundation of relationship. I felt free to open up because I realized everyone else was also trying to sift through their fears and find their identity. I had never felt so accepted in my life. I started to discover that God would peel away the fears and strongholds if I would let Him into those areas to do what He does best – love me. After all, He is love.

"This is a safe, non-judgmental environment where one can be himself and cultivate vulnerability without the fear of being changed by someone."

I know that people aren't perfect, but perfect love is possible. There is a way to create an atmosphere in which those involved are safe to discover and work through fears with the help of Holy Spirit. I know this is true because I am experiencing it. Any time I share what is in my heart, no one ever says, "You shouldn't feel that way," or "That's ridiculous. There's no reason for that." We all give the same honor that we want to receive as we reveal our feelings. Once the fear of judgment is removed, a pathway is created and tools are developed to break down other fears.

Everyone has a desire to be unconditionally loved and fought for. I'm so grateful I have been given a group of people who will encourage me to pursue my dreams, challenge me to go deeper in Jesus, and build me up when I lose hope. I am constantly cultivating a mindset that I can do anything I want because of the love that supports me. This is the type of community that will change the world. This is the Body of Christ living in its full potential. We were created to live in love. Imagine what will happen when a whole generation begins to live fearlessly. We will realize we are dearly loved children and be free to love with our whole hearts!

APPLICATION

Have you experienced an environment in which you felt safe? What was it like?

_____

_____

_____

_____

Do you create an atmosphere of love and safety for the people around you? In what ways?

_____

_____

_____

_____

ACTIVATION

Write down what you could do or be if you were completely fearless. Ignore limitations and ask Holy Spirit for inspiration.

_____

_____

_____

_____

_____

A COMMUNITY OF KINGS
BY: DAVID FRITCH

"And Jonathan, Saul's son, arose and went to David at Horesh, and encouraged him in God. Thus he said to him, "do not be afraid, because the hand of Saul my father will not find you, and you will be king over Israel and I will be next to you."

1 Samuel 23:16-17a, NASB

Recently, God placed a dream in my heart to write a book. As I faced off with the dreaded blank page I was assailed by all the mental enemies that reinforced what I was already feeling inside - "You can't write; you'll never write anything good." As I was sparring with these emotional Nazis, a friend of mine called and without any knowledge of the battle I was in began to encourage and prophesy over my destiny to write a book. His prophecy helped me get in touch with the call of God on my life and the courage that was available to me in Christ. He reminded me of the passion that had been beaten down by discouragement and many failed attempts to write. As soon as I hung up the phone this incredible energy rose up in me, and I wrote for the rest of the day.

Covenant community is about believing in and fighting for the wildest dreams of our brother and sister in Christ's heart. This is the exact opposite of the spirit of the world that only looks out for themselves and demeans and pushes others down in pursuit of success. In the kingdom of God as we serve and sow into the dreams of others God makes a way for us.

"...fights for one another's dream."

The story of Jonathan and David is an astounding picture of what it means to fight for another person's dreams. Jonathan was the heir apparent to his father Saul's throne; yet David was called and anointed by God as the young man to succeed Saul. Most people would have been provoked to a jealous rage, but Jonathan, surprisingly, did the exact opposite. He laid down his right to be king in order to serve the dream of his friend, David. In one of David's most vulnerable times in life, as he was on the run from

Saul, Jonathan reminded him of the call of God on his life to be king and put courage back into his heart.

Jonathan could've pointed out the obvious and said, "David, you are broke, living in caves, and on the run for your life. No one is behind you. You could never be king." Yet, he lifted his eyes above the obvious crisis and failure that David was in and spoke to the truth of his kingly call! Jonathan saw a king in David when others saw a rebellious dissenter. Jonathan's encouragement ultimately prepared the way for David to become king.

Can you imagine living in a group of people that make it a high priority to see each other succeed? What would happen on our campuses, our churches and in our city if we laid down our lives to make each other great? What if everyone around you actually fulfilled their dreams? Could the way we live cultivate and empower a community of kings?

APPLICATION

Can you think of a time when someone saw the call of God in you and encouraged you? How did it make you feel?

_____

_____

_____

_____

_____

ACTIVATION

Get together with your friends and have them share the wildest dreams of their heart. Spend time encouraging them. Then write down 1-2 ways you can fight for your friends dream on a regular basis.

_____

_____

_____

_____

_____

_____

FOUND

BY: COLTON MCHONE

"Let us think of ways to motivate one another to acts of love and good works. And let us not neglect our meeting together, as some people do, but encourage one another, especially now that the day of his return is drawing near."

Hebrews 10:24-25, NLT

In the last few months I have found that being surrounded by people who fully believe in me and fight for the dreams of my heart has allowed me to flourish into who I really am. Being in an environment of community has enabled me to express myself and come before God knowing that He loves me for me and not as anyone else.

A functioning community is a fellowship where every person is enabled to act in their unique gifting and anointing. It's when people come together to edify one another and call out the glory of God they see in each other. It is a place of safety where people can be themselves, uninhibited. Community is about sharing hearts with one another and being vulnerable with each other in every season of the soul. You can show your heart with all of its wounds and scars without any judgment, and only receive love and hope in return. My experience within community is the closest I've seen to the body coming together as one.

"A fellowship of believers unified by and committed to the pursuit of God and love for one another."

This year over Thanksgiving, my wife and I had a few friends over for a feast. The next day one of our friends poured out their heart to us. As I sat there and listened, I realized that this is what Jesus wants from us. He wants us to be there for each other and to open our hearts to one another, just like we open up to Him. Through sharing our hearts with each other we cultivate healing and freedom. I have finally found the community that I have been longing for.

APPLICATION

What does a functioning community look like to you?

_____

_____

_____

_____

_____

_____

_____

_____

How have you been affected by communities in the past? What was good? What was bad?

_____

_____

_____

_____

_____

_____

_____

_____

_____

_____

_____

_____

ACTIVATION

Find someone you trust. Share a piece of your heart with them that you haven't shared before. Meditate on how the connection and conversation went afterwards and see what God was doing through it.

_____

_____

_____

_____

_____

_____

_____

UNIFIED EMPOWERMENT

BY: COURTNEY YATES

"Instead, speaking the truth in love, we will grow to become in every respect the mature body of him who is the head, that is, Christ. From him the whole body, joined and held together by every supporting ligament, grows and builds itself up in love, as each part does its work."

Ephesians 4:15-16

It has always been a dream of mine to dance in a way that causes the enemy to flee. For years I have worshiped this way, but one particular afternoon was very significant in this journey. I was in the prayer room worshipping with my team, and I began to feel a heaviness surrounding me. I felt that my prayers weren't providing the breakthrough I was searching for - I wanted to dance. But I couldn't just get out of my seat because I was simultaneously bombarded by apathy. I began to recognize how I was feeling and thinking and my spirit began to stir inside me. I started seeing images of myself dancing and experiencing the breakthrough that was promised for me and my team. My struggle continued, and I walked to the back of the room seeking some kind of relief.

"It is a community that lives in the light, overcomes struggles and fights for one another's dreams."

As I stood in the back of the room, eyes closed, I cried out for help from the Holy Spirit. When I opened my eyes, I was surprised to see one of my teammates, Daniel, standing right in front of me. He began to share with me that he was seeing a huge angel standing behind me anticipating my next move. He told me, "Do what you want to do, because when you do it there will be breakthrough." His words gave me the strength necessary to push past my emotional dilemma and dance wildly before the Lord. As I responded in worship, the Lord began to lift off the burden I had been feeling.

Daniel knew of this personal dream I had, and his words came exactly when I needed them. He reminded me that I could accomplish what my heart longed for, and my spirit was encouraged to do so. I could believe again that my dancing could truly bring breakthrough in the spiritual realm.

That is what covenant community is all about. It is discovering, recognizing and fighting for the gifts and anointing of others to flow freely. I'm not alone in my fight for the success of my own dreams anymore. I am a part of a beautiful family who can see the gold inside of me and fight for it to be seen by everyone else. Their love gives me the strength and support I need to fulfill the God-given dreams for my life.

APPLICATION

Have you ever been in this kind of community before? If so, describe how your life has changed since you have been in your community. If not, how would you feel about being in this kind of community?

_____

_____

_____

_____

_____

_____

ACTIVATION

Take some time to ask the Lord if there are any dreams you have buried because you have felt alone and hopeless when wanting to pursue them. If so, list them.

_____

_____

_____

_____

Ask the Lord if there are any lies you have believed about being vulnerable in relationships concerning your hopes and dreams. Then ask for truths.

_____

_____

_____

_____

LOVE THAT CHANGES THE WORLD
BY: TANNON HERMAN

"May they be brought to complete unity to let the world know that you sent me and have loved them even as you have loved me."

John 17:23b

Whoa! Wait a second. Did you catch what Jesus just prayed? *Our* unity and love for one another will advance the Gospel to the ends of the earth? Yes, this is the Good News. Jesus left us with two commands to fulfill as believers, and they both boil down to - yep, you guessed it - love. Love is what creates and deepens our communion with God and one another. Love is the substance of God from which we cannot be separated (see Romans 8:38-39). That same love is what Jesus asked God to give to His followers to keep them together. We have been given a love which can keep us from being divided against one another; all we have to do is walk in it.

I have been a part of several teams where church leaders remarked about how they were greatly impacted by our love and unity, but this was recognized on a large scale

"A fellowship of believers unified by and committed to the pursuit of God and love for one another."

for the first time during a Spring Break retreat for young adults in Lynchburg, Virginia. The love seen within our small group of students profoundly impacted the dozens who had joined us for that week. As we began to share this covenantal love with those attending the retreat, all kinds of things began happening: personal breakthroughs, reconciliation of relationships, and increased awareness of the Father's love. Many exclaimed that they had never felt so connected to one another even though they had known each other for years. Others began to revel in the newfound safety they were enjoying in being known and accepted. Yet, overall, everyone was thinking the same thing, "Who else can I share this with?" This is what the love of Christ accomplishes in our hearts.

Just like the core value states, "unified by and committed to," our love for the Lord will bring us together and keep us together. The love of Christ between individuals creates relationships in which we are known but loved, weak but accepted, vulnerable but protected. These unbreakable bonds of covenant are formed in the joint pursuit of relationship with the Father. This kind of love is a gift given to the believer so that the world would know humanity is loved by the Father in the same way He loves the Son.

APPLICATION

Do you think it is possible to love another human being the way the Godhead loves each other? What would that look like?

_____
_____
_____
_____
_____
_____
_____

What does it look like to "love one another" as a mission strategy?

_____
_____
_____
_____
_____
_____
_____
_____

ACTIVATION

God's love is creative. It formed you and knows you. Ask Holy Spirit for creative ways to express your love to those around you today, and then love them!

_____
_____
_____
_____

IT'S TIME FOR WAR!
BY: CRISTINA HERMAN

"Greater love has no one than this, that he lay down his life for his friends."

John 15:13, NIV

One of the greatest expressions of true love is to fight for your brother's dreams. This is a love that can only come from the Father. It is a love that causes us to lay down our lives so that our friends can fulfill their dreams. This is what Jesus did for us. In the same way Jesus fought for us, we should fight for the dreams of our brothers in Christ. The truth about community is that we are one body with one heart and one vision. Yes, we each have our own part, but we are all one. When one part hurts, we all hurt and when one part succeeds, we all share in the victory. When you live in a community that values and really loves one another, fighting for each other's dreams become a natural outflow because their dreams have become your dreams!

"It is a community that...fights for one another's dreams." In my own life, I have experienced this supernatural love to fight for my friends' dreams. About a year ago, some close friends of ours were having a really rough time and were at the point of giving up on their dream to go to Redding, California. Because of the current circumstance, it seemed impossible for them to fulfill this dream. At that moment, something rose up inside of me and said, "No, they must do this!" It was as if their dream became my dream, and I was willing to do anything to help them fulfill it. I felt like we were put in their lives at that very moment to remind them of who they were and what God had called them to do. I knew that this was a fulfillment of walking in community with them and our hearts being knit together. I knew that this was a love that only God could have deposited in my heart for them.

We made sacrifices. It cost us something to really help them fulfill this dream, but it did not seem like a sacrifice at all. It was actually pure joy! A joy I had never quite experienced, until this moment, began to fill my heart. It was then that I knew, to a small degree of, what Hebrews says about Jesus, "who for the joy set before Him endured the cross." There is joy when we lay down our lives to serve the dreams of others. It is a joy only experienced in the outflow of true love and sacrifice made in fighting for the dreams of those whom God has put beside us. I was so grateful and thankful for this moment, because it was in this moment that something in me came alive. Something inside me said, "I was always meant to love like this!"

APPLICATION

Have you ever experienced a situation where someone has fought for your dreams? How did this make you feel?

_____

_____

_____

_____

_____

Have you ever fought for someone else's dream? How did this impact your own life?

_____

_____

_____

_____

_____

ACTIVATION

Take some time to ask the Lord whom He has placed in your life in order for you to fight for their dreams. Talk to this person and share your commitment to them to fight for their dreams. With the Holy Spirit's help, come up with one way that you can actively show that person that you are fighting for their dream. This could be sowing in their dream, encouragement, creatively expressing their dream, praying, or a number of other ways.

_____

_____

_____

_____

_____

_____

Culture of Honor

It is an environment that empowers the individual to live proactively through self-control, responsibility and freedom of choice. Inherent in this culture is the belief that fulfilling the great commission and sustaining revival cannot be fully achieved without interdependence and respect for the diversity of the Body of Christ.

—Core Value #3—

FROM COWER TO POWER

BY: TANNON HERMAN

"Each one should test his own actions. Then he can take pride in himself, without comparing himself to somebody else, for each one should carry his own load."

Galatians 6:4-5

For as long as I can remember I wore the cloak of the "peacekeeper" and disappeared from any situation requiring my opinion. I always felt that to introduce my idea into a conversation would only cause more confusion or tension. This is how I related to life. When a decision was to be made, I ran the other way. When an opinion was required of me I'd simply respond, "I don't really care." The fact is I did care. I always thought my disappearing act was a display of heroic humility, until recently.

"It is an environment that empowers the individual to live proactively through self-control, responsibility and freedom of choice."

The growth I experienced over the past few years has been instrumental in allowing me to really discover "who I am and who I was made to be." That season began a little rocky as I would cowardly deflect any opportunity to look inside of myself. My blindness was my defense. As long as I was unaware of what was going on inside of me, I didn't feel responsible to do anything about it. But my wall of bliss came tumbling down as I learned the discipline of partnering with the Lord to examine my heart. While co-laboring with the Man who laid down his life for me, I saw what He saw - a powerful man. My faulty self-perspective, perpetuated by a cycle of powerlessness, was dashed to pieces and a new man, the real me, rose up through it all.

This new man, this new me, wasn't afraid anymore. I understood for the first time that I am in control of me, and no one else is. In fact, I also realized I was not in control of anyone else, either. I was set free from the anxiety of trying to predict everyone's reactions to my life. I laid down the fear that had convinced me it was my job to either become invisible or make others invisible through controlling them. Paul instructed the church members in

Galatia to "carry [your] own load." (Galatians 6:5) He understood the principle of the Kingdom which says, "I am in control of me, and you are in control of you."

It is in this freedom of self-control that we are empowered to live purposefully and without fear of others. Jesus died to preserve free will, the most precious of gifts to humanity. It is the freedom to choose for ourselves. We can no longer pretend that we don't have a choice. What are you doing with yours?

APPLICATION

Do you feel that you are in control of your life? Why or why not?

_____

_____

_____

_____

What does it mean to "live proactively through self-control, responsibility and freedom of choice?"

_____

_____

_____

_____

_____

ACTIVATION

Are there any relationships in your life in which you feel that you "disappear" or take control? Write down some ways you can begin to exercise self-control in those relationships.

_____

_____

_____

_____

_____

_____

_____

_____

HONOR BUILDS BRIDGES
BY: DAVID FRITCH

"Anyone who receives a prophet because he is a prophet will receive a prophet's reward"

Matthew. 10:41a

Several years ago I was at a revival service designed to draw people from many different churches. While the worship was going on, I was fighting disappointment and frustration for the lack of participation from local congregations. In that moment, the Holy Spirit suddenly came on me and I saw the strategy of the enemy to divide the church through dishonor.

I saw that each church had stronger gifts and anointing in certain areas such as evangelism or the prophetic. Because of the grace on their lives for these gifts, they were measuring and judging other believers and churches that weren't as strong as they were. Then the Lord said to me, "The Church has become weak because they have not honored one another." God began to pierce my own heart and revealed to me how I had also judged other believers by the standard of my own gifting. As I repented, it was as if my eyes were opened to see the beauty in the diversity of the body of Christ for the first time. I was grieved that I had built walls against other believers through my dishonor. Dishonor creates barriers, but honor builds bridges where we have access to the anointing on one another's lives.

"Inherent in this culture is the belief that fulfilling the great commission and sustaining revival cannot be fully achieved without interdependence and respect for the diversity of the Body of Christ."

The people that found it the most difficult to honor Jesus were the ones from His own hometown. Jesus' friends and family couldn't see past His earthly nature and occupation, and as a result, "He could not do any miracles there" (Mk. 6:5). When Jesus went to other towns they didn't see a carpenter, but they saw and honored Him as a great prophet and healer. Their honor released Jesus to perform many mighty miracles. Dishonor keeps us focused on people's weaknesses, but honor causes us to see their strengths.

When we honor others for who they are and what God has given them then we will receive of their anointing and be blessed and strengthened. Matthew 10:41 records, "Anyone who receives a prophet because he is a prophet will receive a prophet's reward." What blessings and outpourings have we missed because we have not honored the family of God? What could God do in our cities, and even within the walls of our own churches, if we would look past each other's weaknesses and honor the gift of God? Let's find out!

APPLICATION

Ask the Holy Spirit to show you if you have dishonored anyone around you. As He shows you take time to repent.

_____

_____

_____

_____

ACTIVATION

Write down the name of a church you are not a part of but you know something about. Write down what negative perceptions you have had of them. Ask God to you show you what He sees in them. Then write an encouraging note and mail it to the pastor of that church.

_____

_____

_____

_____

_____

_____

_____

_____

_____

_____

_____

_____

_____

_____

YOUR CHOICE

BY: JOSHUA SWARNY

> "It is for freedom that Christ has set us free. Stand firm, then, and do not let yourselves be burdened again by a yoke of slavery."
>
> Galatians 5:1

Just as Paul said, Christ died so that we may be *free*. Through His life and death, Jesus completely destroyed the bondage of sin and provided us a way to live again as God originally intended. We were created with a free will – a necessary element for us to make our own decisions. The risk in our design is that we have equal capacity of choosing sin as we do obedience to God; however, without the freedom of choice being placed inside our hearts, we could never decided to honor and love God.

I used to think that God wanted to control me. Why would I not want Him to? After all, He knows best, right? My mindset was to lay down my freedom and rights so I could be sure God would take control of my life. The problem is: God does not want to control me. He created us with a spirit of self-control, and when that ability was compromised by sin He immediately planned to redeem that gift to us. I was liberated by this revelation because I realized God created me to enjoy me, not control me. He actually wants me! His desire wasn't to have a family of robots; He wanted real people, real lovers, like Himself.

I am learning that God has also given me this freedom for my relationships with other people. I grew up under a pressure of trying to fulfill every expectation placed on me, which is also known as the fear of man. I am made to meet peoples' needs, but it was never God's intention that I become a slave to others' expectations.

This revelation became more real to me than ever during a summer mission trip with the Burning Ones Mission Base called the Burn Wagon.

"It is an environment that empowers the individual to live proactively through self-control, responsibility and freedom of choice."

While on the trip, I discovered the Lord loved who I was and wanted me for me. What I experienced on the trip was a community reflecting true love and covenant between believers. Living in an environment like this for three weeks empowered me to be myself around others. I felt like whatever choice I wanted to make, I had the power to make it.

I am now beginning to understand I was made with the power of choice. Each day I am exercising this responsibility more and more, and I am continually being transformed by His freely given freedom for my life.

APPLICATION

What, if any, areas of bondage are you in or have been in?

_____

_____

_____

_____

How do you feel about being free, and thus being responsible for your actions?

_____

_____

_____

_____

ACTIVATION

Spend time with the Lord and ask Him what He enjoys about you? Journal about it.

_____

_____

_____

_____

Practice owning the choices you make throughout the day no matter how big or small they are, and journal about how it made you feel.

_____

_____

_____

_____

_____

LESSONS IN LOVING
BY: COLTON MCHONE

"Beloved, let us love one another, for love is from God, and whoever loves has been born of God and knows God. Anyone who does not love does not know God, because God is love."

1 John 4:7-8

For my entire life I've struggled with being judgmental and critical of others. Because of my own insecurities and hurts, I've had trouble getting to know people or opening myself up to others. My judgments towards others prevented me from really getting to know my brothers and sisters in the Body of Christ. My opportunities to connect and bond with several people were extremely limited because of my attitude toward the world.

A few months ago, I lived in a town in western Oklahoma where I was very different from the people around me. I discovered a huge lack in connection between big city and small town culture, so I didn't make many close friends while I was there. Looking back, I realize that my lack of connection stemmed from my unwillingness to let go of my own pride and learn to enjoy those I was surrounded by. I didn't let anyone in and in return felt very lonely and isolated.

"...revival cannot be fully achieved without interdependence and respect for the diversity of the Body of Christ."

I really wish I had opened up and let people in. If I had just laid aside my differences, I might have made lifelong friends or encountered people who would have shared their hearts with me. But because I didn't, the majority of my memories from that season are filled with loneliness and depression.

I learned how important it is to honor those around me, even if they are different from me. That at times it is necessary to put aside my own customs and way of life to get to know God's children. His heart is longing and full of love for every person on this planet. I want to walk in that same kind of love. I long to see His children through His eyes, not from my own jaded perception. My desire is to honor people and their cultures, and not just those in a foreign country, but the people right in front of me.

APPLICATION

Was there ever a time when you kept someone at a distance because of your judgments or insecurities?

_____

_____

_____

_____

_____

How do you think that affected you? How do you think that affected them?

_____

_____

_____

_____

_____

ACTIVATION

Spend some time with Father God and ask Him to help you let down the walls that keep you from getting to know His children. Write down what He tells you. Make a plan to get to know someone new today.

_____

_____

_____

_____

_____

_____

_____

_____

_____

_____

_____

_____

_____

OUT OF CONTROL
BY: CRISTINA HERMAN

"For God gave us a spirit not of fear but of power and love and self-control."

2 Timothy 1:7, ESV

For the longest time, although sometimes unaware, I have dealt with fear. This fear led me to control my environment, people, or whatever was necessary in order to protect myself. I did not know how to control myself so I tried to control others to get my needs met. I blamed others for my problems and never took responsibility for my own actions. My lack of self-control in the midst of strong emotions has led to great heartache, a lot of shame and caused others much pain.

Of course I would feel *bad* for how I had acted and what I did afterwards but feeling bad wasn't enough. This process of acting out of control, feeling sorry and then going back and repeating the same actions continued. I thought I had repented but real repentance requires a change of direction. Because I never fully took ownership for my lack of self-control, I was stuck in the same cycle and a "victim" to my own emotions.

"It is an environment that empowers the individual to live proactively through self-control, responsibility and freedom of choice."

As the Lord healed my heart, I began to get breakthrough in this area. I started to see that because of my brokenness I saw everyone and their actions through the lenses of rejection. This lense clouded my view and I was unable to see people for who they really were. The more that He healed my heart the more I saw that my actions needed to change, and they did to an extent. I had less and less outbreaks of out-of-control anger and more and more victories. But the real breakthrough happened when I finally took full responsibility for my actions.

I learned that I have a choice to make everyday. No matter what others do to me, I am responsible for how I act. I am responsible to control myself. I cannot control others and no one can control me. Because of what Jesus did on the cross I now have the power to control myself and how I respond in any given situation. This is self-control; He has overcome, so I too can overcome.

I am only at the beginning of a beautiful journey of walking in self-control. Fear continues to leave my life as this revelation goes deeper and deeper into my heart. His grace is there to empower me to walk this out daily. His Love is filling my heart, home and relationships; a perfect love that casts out all fear.

APPLICATION

Do you struggle controlling yourself in the midst of great emotions? Why or why not?

_____

_____

_____

_____

In what ways do you struggle with trying to control others? Ask the Father to bring His love to cast out the fear and give you truth.

_____

_____

_____

_____

_____

ACTIVATION

Take some time to write down a plan of action of how you will respond the next time others push your buttons. Be as specific as possible and address the areas you have trouble using self-control.

_____

_____

_____

_____

_____

_____

_____

_____

IRONING OUT OUR DIFFERENCES
BY: MICHELLE SMITH

"As iron sharpens iron, so one man sharpens another."

Proverbs 27:17. NIV

After graduating high school, I packed up my little two-door Nissan Sentra and moved across the country to the promised land, also known as California. In my 18-year-old mind, I was living the dream. It was my first time moving away from home and also my first time having roommates and sharing a bedroom. I moved in with three young women who I had never met before, and I quickly discovered that they didn't do things the way that I did things.

My roommate was a missionary kid who had grown up in the Philippines in an environment where she literally shared everything. In my mind she had absolutely no boundaries, and it infuriated me when I saw her at class wearing my jewelry and clothes without asking, or eating the food that I had purchased with the few extra dollars I had. I was absolutely offended, and because I refused to communicate in a healthy way there was no resolution to what was escalating into a huge rift in our relationship.

"Inherent in this culture is the belief that fulfilling the great commission… cannot be fully achieved without interdependence and respect for the diversity of the Body of Christ."

When we finally spoke about the problems that had developed, I quickly realized that I, too, was offending her by my behavior. Because we didn't communicate our needs to each other, dissention had grown to the point of division. Shortly after our conversation, the tension that I constantly felt around her began to lift, and we were able to enjoy the friendship that we were meant to have.

It was only through differences and disagreements that I was able to learn from my roommate. She had a deep understanding of community dynamics that I had never experienced before and that I certainly did not understand. Through healthy communication and learning to embrace her, I began to understand how one man (or, in this case, woman) can sharpen another.

For iron to sharpen iron, an abrasive point of contact is required. Somehow I always interpreted this scripture as a painless and disagreement-free process of growing with others. The reality, however, is the process of sharpening and being sharpened is absolutely transformative. What I have learned from this scripture and my experiences is that God is interested in the process of bringing us into respectful relationships that are marked by the honor we show one another. His purpose is not for every believer to agree with everything but to fully embrace the differences that we all have and to allow those to be tools that sharpen us and our relationship with Him.

APPLICATION

How do you generally respond to conflict in relationship? Why?

_____

_____

_____

_____

_____

_____

ACTIVATION

Can you identify an experience that felt like offense, but was really the Lord using another person to "sharpen" you? How could you have better responded?

_____

_____

_____

_____

_____

_____

_____

_____

Paradigm of Hope

This is an approach to life rooted in the goodness of a loving, all-powerful God. It is where one's heart is anchored in hope and fully awakened to the endless possibilities that God's goodness can and will break out at any moment. This perspective cultivates both creativity and a dreaming heart, which is vital for establishing the Kingdom of God in the earth.

—Core Value #4—

HISTORY IS WRITTEN BY DREAMERS
BY: DAVID FRITCH

"...a dream fulfilled is a tree of life."

Proverbs 13:12b, NLT

Several years ago on a ministry trip to Arkansas I met a ten-year-old girl whose simple, faith-filled words shifted the entire direction of my life. One night after dinner I asked her what she wanted to do when she grew up and she said, "I want to be a hairstylist, end child slavery, and start orphanages all over the world." I was amused she had so casually put being a hairstylist in the same category with such heroic acts of justice, but I was more so in awe of her simple faith that her dream could actually happen. God began to show me how I had stopped dreaming and how we as believers are called to live in an atmosphere of hope. To have hope is to live in perpetual expectancy of the goodness of God breaking out.

History was written by dreamers. Every great movement, successful business, and justice initiative was catalyzed by ordinary people with an awe-inspiring picture of the future. Where would our generation be without men like the Wright brothers, Albert Einstein, and Martin Luther King Jr.? These men practiced the art of dreaming and changed history. Dreamers see what others cannot see and therefore do what others will not do.

"It is where one's heart is anchored in hope and fully awakened to the endless possibilities that God's goodness can and will break out at any moment."

What are we dreaming about today that will change the way the next generation lives? Is it possible that the next generation could never know the apathy, indifference, and barrenness of the church of today? Could it be possible when those who are five years old now turn twenty-five that abortion could be abolished, sex trafficking ended, and the pornography industry bankrupted? Could it be possible that in twenty years, AIDS and cancer will only be distant memories and stories we tell our children? Could it be possible that we could receive a revelation from Heaven so big that it ignites revival movements in cities, campuses, and churches that sweep millions into the kingdom of God?

It blows my mind to think that what we write in our journals today could alter the course of nations tomorrow. The earth is groaning and waiting for sons of the most-high God to step into the fullness of who they are. To not discover, cultivate, and act on your dreams is to rob the next generation of breakthrough. What are you dreaming about?

APPLICATION

Do you feel you are living in an atmosphere of hope and expectancy? Why or why not?

_____
_____
_____

ACTIVATION

Ask yourself what you would do with your life and how you would want to impact the world if you didn't have any fear or limitations? Write down at least 10 dreams and begin to pray over them daily.

_____
_____
_____
_____
_____

1. _____
2. _____
3. _____
4. _____
5. _____
6. _____
7. _____
8. _____
9. _____
10. _____

HOPE WAITS

BY: COURTNEY NICHOLE YATES

"I wait for the Lord, my whole being waits, and in His word I put my hope."

Psalms 130:5

A few months before I started the Burning Ones Discipleship School, I went through a season where the Lord stripped everything away, so that He could teach me to be fully dependant on Him. He even led me to let go of the ownership of my car to my ex-boyfriend. The Lord had spoken clearly to me, "Let it go, it is just a car. I will provide for you." This was a hard word, but because the Lord had spoken so clearly, I simply obeyed.

About 6 months later, in the middle of the Discipleship School, my leader David asked me, "Are you praying for a car?" "No, I hadn't thought about it honestly", I responded to him. "Well you should start praying for one. Over the years, God has supernaturally provided me a car whenever I needed one. He can do the same for you if you just ask Him."

My journey of praying and hoping in God's goodness had begun. Suddenly, everywhere we went I would meet people who had similar stories. They would tell me their testimonies of how the Lord provided a vehicle for them, encouraging me that God could do the same for me. Every time the flame of hope in my heart was beginning to grow dim, God would lead me to people who would share testimonies of God's supernatural provision. The words they spoke would fan the flame of hope that the Lord was anchoring in my heart and I once again would be encouraged.

"It is where one's heart is anchored in hope and fully awakened to the endless possibilities that God's goodness can and will break out at any moment."

The Discipleship school ended and I still hadn't received a car. I was desperate. I now needed a car more than ever. My family told me all the things that I needed to do in order to get a car. I tried to take it into my own hands and became very anxious and stressed out. Later I repented for trying to do it in my own strength, as the Lord reminded me of what He had said, that He would provide. So there I was clinging to the hope and belief that God is good all the time. I chose to believe that His words are true and will always come to pass.

On October 2nd of 2012, ten months after having that conversation with David, I received a phone call from him. "Hello, Courtney! I have exciting news for you!" "You do?" I said anxiously. "The Lord has heard your prayers for a car; my brother's in-laws would like to give you their old car!" The Lord had once again proven Himself good and faithful. He heard my prayers and saw the hope I had in my heart for this request. The Lord led this couple to *give* me their car. And to prove that God has a sense of humor, their last name is Love.

APPLICATION

Was there ever a time in your life when you put your hope in God for something? What happened as a result?

_____

_____

_____

ACTIVATION

Spend some time with the Lord and search your heart. Ask Him these questions and write down what He shows you.

"Father, is there any place in my heart where I have allowed hopelessness to set in?"

_____

_____

Father, are their any lies that I have believed about You regarding hope?

_____

_____

What truth do you want to give me about you in place of those lies?

_____

_____

Now take some time to repent for agreeing with these lies and thank Him for the truth He gave you!

MISSION: ACCOMPLISHED
BY: MICHELLE SMITH

"And the LORD answered me: 'Write the vision; make it plain on tablets, so he may run who reads it.'"

Habakkuk 2:2, ESV

Since I became a Christian at age 17, I've been an avid journaler, documenting virtually every event in my life. Whether they were dreams I had at night, or dreams of what I felt called to in the future, there are pages and lists of dreams scattered through all of my journals.

In the summer of 2012, I took some time to read through my journals to remember what God has done in my life. It was an incredible journey full of thanksgiving as I recollected the countless times that God has been completely faithful to me.

One of the most striking things that I noticed was how quickly God responded to the desires of my heart after I took time to write them down. In one of my

"This perspective cultivates... a dreaming heart, which is vital for establishing the Kingdom of God in the earth."

journals from 2010, I had a dream list of about 12 things, including: experiencing restoration in my relationship with my parents, studying abroad, living in Israel, and being a part of building a house of prayer in the nations. Just two years later, every dream on that list has been accomplished.

At that time, I was dreaming the biggest dreams I could. I didn't have the capacity to dream more than what I had written down. Because I have seen all of those dreams accomplished, my current dreams are bigger than I could ever have imagined just a few years earlier. Without dreaming those dreams, writing them down, and believing that God is faithful to accomplish them, I probably wouldn't have seen them come into fruition.

The principle from Habakkuk shows us how powerful it is not only to dream and have a vision, but to actually write it down. God certainly knows our hearts, but when the vision is written down, there is a tangible substance to it, and therefore, an accountability. God never forgets our dreams, and He wants us to live full of hope and expectation for the fulfillment of every desire He has placed in our hearts.

APPLICATION

Write down dreams that you have already seen God accomplish in your life. Give Him thanks! If there is a place where you have written down your dreams, review it and see what God has done.

_____

_____

_____

_____

_____

_____

ACTIVATION

Take some time to dream today. Write down every dream that comes to mind - even those that seem impossible to you! Spend 15-20 minutes writing. Revisit this list in 6 months, 1 year, or 2 years. Rejoice in all that God has done!

_____

_____

_____

_____

_____

_____

_____

_____

_____

_____

_____

_____

_____

_____

_____

_____

_____

_____

TODAY'S THE DAY!

BY: CODY MYERS

"Hope deferred makes the heart sick, but a dream fulfilled is a tree of life."

Proverbs 13:12, ESV

One of the most beautiful things God has done in my heart is igniting hope. My hope had been buried and I was trying to replace it with what I thought was faith, but was really just a cover for my disappointment. I had head knowledge that God would bring revival to our nation, and heal the sick in our city, but I had no expectation that He was yearning to do it now and wanted my partnership in His reign of love.

I remember a worship set one morning in the Burning Ones Discipleship School of 2012. One of the leaders, Tannon, was flowing in a prophetic song and singing, "Today's the day!" We began to pray and sing this phrase over our city with the mindset that revival and reformation could happen right now even in what seemed a hopeless region.

"...one's heart is...fully awakened to the endless possibilities that God's goodness can and will break out at any moment."

Since this experience, "Today's the day," and "why not today?" stuck with me and I began declaring these sayings over my life, my family, my finances, my healing - anything and everything I could think of. I began to expect His goodness to break out at any moment. Father God transformed my mind and heart as I realized that the impossible could happen at any time because everything is possible with God, and Jesus is my hope! It even became normal in the Burning Ones to randomly shout, "Today's the day!" when discussing the goodness of God.

Healing the sick and moving in the supernatural has since become a normal part of my life. My whole paradigm has been transformed by this reality. I truly believe that everyday is a day to be expectant. Everyday is a day to see what God is up to. The message of hope is one I will never tire of passing on.

APPLICATION

Why is hope an important part of our walk with Christ?

_____

_____

_____

_____

What impact do we have on the lives of others when we carry hope?

_____

_____

_____

_____

Have you been an ambassador of hope? How?

_____

_____

_____

_____

ACTIVATION

Think over your life and ask the Lord if you've settled into hopelessness. Ask Him to reveal where it crept in and let Him guide you through healing. Ask Jesus to restore hope again in your life. Don't forget to write about this experience so you can be filled with hope again and again!

_____

_____

_____

_____

_____

_____

_____

_____

_____

_____

_____

_____

HOPE IN A ZIPLOC BAG

BY: TANNON HERMAN

"The one who calls you is faithful and He will do it."

1 Thessalonians 5:24

Have you ever been in a situation where you have been pounding Heaven with all your muster and might to no avail? Or maybe you felt like a situation was literally impossible? I find it difficult to believe the Lord would keep anyone from these circumstances simply because of what happens inside of our hearts in moments like these. Let's face it - the Lord loves opportunities to show Himself off to the world. There is nothing better than to be a part of these magnificent displays of faithfulness.

In my lifetime I have had the privilege of enjoying several of these moments. As a sixteen year-old I had planned to be in Thailand for two months during the summer. I had been on several trips before so I didn't think anything of the $5500 price tag that accompanied this adventure. God had always come through for me. But this year, this time, it was different. None of the usual fundraising tricks were working. No one seemed interested in what I was doing. I remember thinking "Why isn't anyone giving anything? Did I do something wrong? God, do you even care?" It was one of the most frustrating seasons I had ever experienced, but a glimmer of light was in the distance.

"This is an approach to life rooted in the goodness of a loving, all-powerful God."

I sat down in my bedroom with my guitar that I barely knew how to play and began to sing out my frustrations to the Lord. Quickly, though, my accusations against the Lord were greeted with violent opposition from an old friend, Hope. Hope invaded my bedroom and enabled me to lift my eyes up from the issue-at-hand to see the Father's heart. As I began to agree with what hope was accomplishing in my heart a new wave of faith flooded my soul.

Weeks later, I showed up at the training site for my team with a ziploc bag filled with $6500, most of it given to me hours before I left home. I could feel the love and power of the Father as He laughed from the heavens. Since that day my heart has learned to expect His goodness. When others feel like giving up or slowing down, I just wait. Hope will carry me.

APPLICATION

What situations in your life need to encounter the spirit of hope?

_____

_____

_____

_____

_____

_____

_____

_____

_____

_____

Is there a time in your life that you feel like God "showed off" His goodness towards you. What happened and how did this make you feel?

_____

_____

_____

_____

_____

_____

_____

_____

_____

_____

_____

ACTIVATION

Grab your journal and find a place to be alone with God. Begin to dialogue with the Lord about any areas of frustration you might have in your relationship with Him. Afterwards, give thanks for those times He has reminded you of when He came through for you.

WEARING HEAVEN'S LENSES
BY: CRISTINA HERMAN

"...Christ in you, the hope of Glory."

Colossians. 1:27b

Hope is living from Heaven to Earth; it is wearing the lenses of Heaven everyday as we live on this earth. It is being rooted in the perspective that we have the victory and ability to overcome because He overcame. It is the belief that nothing is impossible and everything is possible. It is the position of our hearts that chooses to believe He is truly good all the time. Hope is where the impossible blooms, dreams are birthed and the supernatural thrives.

In my own life I have been on a journey of living life through Heaven's lenses. Hopelessness was something familiar to me. Every time we left our city, Shawnee, and came back from a trip, hopelessness would suddenly fill my heart. Over time I began to recognize it but this was not enough. I needed to overcome it! This happened time and time again. The same discouragement would come my way and I would give in to it not realizing that by forfeiting my hope I was partnering with the enemy.

"It is where one's heart is anchored in hope and fully awakened to the endless possibilities that God's goodness can and will break out at any moment."

After this summer's mission trip, the BurnWagon, there was a shift that took place in my life. Hope began rooting itself in my heart. After seeing more than 100 healings, including legs growing out and creative miracles, my perspective changed. Living in the realm of the supernatural for three weeks transformed my mind. When I came home, the light bulb came on: I did not have to live in hopelessness anymore! I realized the choice was there all along to agree with hope or hopelessness every morning. I could overcome this atmosphere! I could not only overcome it, but change my city through my agreement with Heaven.

I made a choice to partner with hope and out of this place new life began to flow. I began to fight for the destiny of my city, instead of giving into what seemed familiar. From this place I began declaring the provision of Heaven and for the supernatural to be released and God began to move and answer those prayers in a tangible way. We continue to experience an outflow from what had occurred on that summer trip: healings, miracles and breakthrough.

Jesus is Hope itself. So, if He lives in me I am anchored in Hope. It is only a matter of choice: will I choose hope or will I listen to discouragement? Will I put on Heaven's lenses today or will I partner with what I see in the natural? This is something that I contend with daily. There are unlimited resources at our fingertips. Will we release them to others or will we keep them locked away? The choice is ours today. Hope is knocking at the door of your heart. What will you do?

APPLICATION

Do you struggle with hopelessness? If so, in what ways?

_____

_____

_____

Ask the Holy Spirit to expose any lies you have believed that have their root in hopelessness. Ask Him to give you the truth in place of those lies.

_____

_____

ACTIVATION

Dream with the Lord about what you could do with the unlimited resources of Heaven. What could happen in your life? What could happen in your city? Your nation? Find a way to act on what you've written down, today!

_____

_____

_____

_____

_____

_____

_____

Restoration
of the Heart

The heart of man is the treasure of the Lord and His desire is to see His people completely healed and established as sons and daughters. We believe that discipleship is a journey of the heart, which involves renewing the mind, deliverance from strongholds, and inner-healing. The unconditional love experienced through God and covenantal community creates a safe environment for restoration of the heart.

—Core Value #5—

BE MADE WHOLE

BY: CODY MYERS

"And a certain man was there, which had an infirmity thirty and eight years. When Jesus saw him...and knew that he had been now a long time in that case, He saith unto him, Wilt thou be made whole?"

John 5:5-6, KJV

In this passage, Jesus is asking permission to restore this man. I would like to think that Jesus wouldn't have to ask. Doesn't everyone want to be whole? Doesn't everyone want to be healed? The idea of being healed inside and out was what I longed for, but I never knew how much healing I really needed. The insecurities I was hanging onto were hindering me from being restored to the daughter I was created to be.

I grew up second-to-youngest in a very large family. I thought I was okay with standing back and letting everyone else have their moment. In my mind, it was better "not to be a burden" and stay out of the way. I was absolutely loved and cared for, but I had a problem voicing what my heart needed because I didn't want to make anyone's life more difficult. What I didn't realize was that by stuffing my feelings and not making my needs known, I was damaging my own heart.

"...His desire is to see His people completely healed..."

The Lord desired to show me my own value, so He took me away from what was familiar and placed me in a culture that highly values authenticity and vulnerability. This community made it safe for me to share my heart and voice my needs. I was now in the position of the man in John 5. My weaknesses and issues were being exposed and Jesus was asking if I wanted to be made whole. Through the Scriptures and teachings I received, I began to realize how much my Father treasured me and that I could share my heart with Him.

I chose to trust Him with the deepest parts of my life and little by little, He healed each hurt as it surfaced. Every time I was vulnerable and let Him see into me, He proved that the safest place for my heart was in His hands. He waited until I was ready and then flooded my innermost being with grace, mercy, and love. He helped me tear down strongholds that had kept me from being myself. He replaced those strongholds with true perceptions of who He is and who I am.

Jesus asked me rather than just barging in because He wanted to show me that my voice matters. He was thrilled to be my answer, as soon as I wanted Him to be. He gave me the opportunity to truly believe in Him and watch Him come through. I am so glad He loves me into wholeness.

APPLICATION

Do you think Jesus can and wants to make you whole? Why or why not?

How would your outlook on life change if you were made completely whole? What would you do differently?

ACTIVATION

Take some time to get alone with Jesus and ask Him to show you the areas in which He wants to love you into wholeness over the next season of your life. Write down what He says to you. Express to Him your fears or concerns so He can assure you that you are safe.

PERFECT IN LOVE

BY: JOSHUA SWARNY

"There is no fear in love; but perfect love casts out fear, because fear involves torment. But he who fears has not been made perfect in love."

1 Jn 4:18, NKJV

The more I search the scriptures I find kingdom life is all about love. The Word says, "God is love" (1 Jn 4:8). If God is love and God is infinite, meaning without boundaries, then I believe love is the same. The depths and reality of love and what that looks like are limitless. There are no boundaries love cannot cross. We cannot earn the love of God, so we cannot "un-earn" His love. This is unconditional love; it is perfect love and it creates a safe environment.

"The unconditional love experienced through God and covenantal community creates a safe environment for restoration of the heart."

In environments where there is punishment, fear has opportunity to become the driving force of our lives. Where there is punishment, we respond out of fear of physical or emotional pain. This fear driven environment diminishes the matters of the heart, leaving hurts, wounds and insecurities unattended, causing us to engage in a survival mentality to get our needs met by any means necessary. This unhealthy lifestyle reveals that our hearts need to be restored to the Creator, who intended for us to live in love.

The Lord's government is a government of love. He took the punishment for us in order to display how important our hearts are to Him. The Father took joy in loving us instead of bringing punishment for our sinful actions. He wants to restore our hearts to life. Though I have desired to live like this, I haven't felt empowered to do so until recently with the Burning Ones Missions Base community. In this family of believers, I have opened my heart before God while allowing others to see inside of me. I have rarely felt safe before this to open my heart in front of others. If I had kept my heart closed, I would never have seen the fear, timidity and false humility in me and never dealt with it.

A safe place is created through love which enables hearts to be restored by encountering the perfect love of Christ. The Lord desires for us to be made perfect in love and create a place where love reigns over fear.

APPLICATION

How do you think love creates a safe place? Do you believe your heart would be healed in an environment of unconditional love?

_____

_____

_____

_____

_____

_____

_____

_____

_____

_____

_____

_____

ACTIVATION

Write and compare your experiences of living out of fear and living out of love. Observe the impact each had on your life.

_____

_____

_____

_____

_____

_____

_____

_____

_____

_____

ACHIEVING TO RECEIVING

BY: CRISTINA HERMAN

"He makes me to lie down in green pastures. He leads me beside the still waters. He restores my soul..."

Psalms 23:2-3, NKJV

In 2009, the summer after I did the Burning Ones Discipleship School, I spent hours looking for a job and every place I applied to resulted in a dead end. I continued to search for ways to stay busy because I felt empty and purposeless. As long as I was not producing anything I felt worthless. But the Lord had a purpose in all of this. He wanted to break me out of this destructive cycle of finding my identity in my accomplishments and bring restoration to my weary soul. My Good Shepherd was leading me to lie down in green pastures and sit beside quiet waters, and I was doing everything I could to resist this process.

After continuing my desperate search for a job, I finally gave in to the leading of my good Father. He showed me He was trying to restore my heart with a season of sitting at His feet. It was only in stripping away my false comfort in achievement that the Lord was able to bring the real healing and comfort that I needed. He was more concerned with mending my heart than about me producing something for Him.

"The heart of man is the treasure of the Lord and His desire is to see His people completely healed..."

Out of simply being with the Lord, healing began to flow to the broken places of my heart. I wrote more songs and received more revelation during that time than ever before. That season bore fruit that I am still experiencing today. On the outside, that time of my life looked barren and foolish in the eyes of the world - but in His eyes, it was beautiful and fruitful because I was receiving the restoration I desperately needed.

This is how healing of our hearts often comes. God takes us to a place of rest; a time to be still, listen and simply receive. We have to be quiet enough to let the thoughts, hurts and brokenness come to the surface. When we are taken away from the things we use to numb the pain in our hearts, real transformation can begin to take place.

APPLICATION

Ask the Holy Spirit, "Are there any false comforts that I use to medicate my pain? If so, what are they?"

_____

_____

_____

_____

_____

_____

In what ways is God trying to strip these false comforts away?

_____

_____

_____

_____

_____

_____

ACTIVATION

Take 30 minutes to simply be with the Lord. Let Him lead you to quiet waters and restore broken places in your heart. Don't do anything during this time, but simply listen to His voice and be with Him. Afterwards, write down what the Lord showed you.

_____

_____

_____

_____

_____

_____

_____

_____

_____

_____

THE BEGINNING PLACE OF FREEDOM
BY: DAVID FRITCH

"How foolish can you be? After starting your Christian lives in the Spirit, why are you now trying to become perfect by your own human effort?"

Galatians 3:3, NLT

The summer after I graduated from high school my family rented a condo on the Gulf Coast for one month. I was eighteen, trying to walk with God, but I was miserable. My life in God was an obligation rather than a joy, and a set of rules instead of a relationship. The importance of having a daily prayer time was hammered into me by my pastors and youth leaders as the key to Christian growth, and so I zealously pursued this. When I didn't fulfill my duty I felt like God was angry at me and that I didn't deserve to be used by Him. I lived under a weight of constant guilt and shame, and prayer seemed to be the biggest burden of all.

During this time it was my daily routine to try and pray for two hours. I remember taking walks on the beach and counting down the minutes until my dreaded prayer time was over. One day after I returned from my seaside prayer walk the scripture reference Galatians 3:3 popped into my head. I had no idea what it said, but I thought maybe God was trying to speak to me. When I read the verse out loud the truth of it smashed my heart and instantly set me free from the massive weight of guilt I was carrying.

"The unconditional love experienced through God ... creates a safe environment for the restoration of the heart."

The verse said, "How foolish can you be? After starting your Christian lives in the Spirit, why are you now trying to become perfect by your own human effort" (Gal. 3:3)? I realized in that moment I was trying to earn the free gift of God's love by all my good works and extensive prayer times. God was showing me He wasn't interested in my human effort, but He wanted me to know the depth of His love and the price He already paid for me to be free. Understanding how much God loved me in my weakness was the beginning place of freedom.

God is committed to us and loves us on our best and our worst day. He doesn't give up on us because we struggle. This revelation sets us free from guilt, shame and needless striving. Ask the Lord to open your eyes to see how much He loves you and watch what happens to your life.

APPLICATION

Do you feel like you are trying to earn God's love? Why or why not?

_____

_____

_____

_____

_____

ACTIVATION

Ask God to forgive you for trusting in your own strength rather than the price He paid on the cross. Then, ask the Holy Spirit to show you what the Father thinks and feels about you? Write down what you see, hear or feel.

_____

_____

_____

_____

_____

_____

_____

_____

_____

_____

_____

_____

_____

_____

_____

_____

IDENTITY
BY: COLTON MCHONE

"Here on earth you will have many trials and sorrows. But take heart, because I have overcome the world."

John: 16:33, NLT

When I was a baby, due to some tricky circumstances and a few unfortunate events, my father was not able to be in my life. He didn't know that I was his son, so he went on to live his own life. I certainly don't fault him for this, but it did mark the course for my life. From that point on, I embarked on a journey of my own heart in finding God and God finding me.

Because I grew up without a father, I had an unformed identity, meaning I didn't have a dad to validate and affirm who I was. This launched me into a life of searching for my identity. My life became about finding freedom and searching for the truth of who I am. I would try to find my identity in what I wore or whom I surrounded myself with, but in the end I still felt lost and hopeless.

When I was close to 19 years old, I attended a prayer meeting that changed my life. I had never really *"We believe that discipleship is a journey of the heart..."* heard of a supernatural lifestyle and had no clue of what it meant. At the end of the meeting, one of the leaders started praying for me. He invited Jesus to come and remove the hurts of my past. In that moment I felt a literal rush of water fall on me. It was full of love, mercy, and grace. Then I heard Jesus whisper in my ear over and over, "I love you." After all of this happened, Jesus began restoring my heart from the past hurts of my father and other things I had dealt with.

He is still restoring my heart, chasing after me and pursuing me in every moment. He hasn't stopped and He never will. I'm so amazed by what Jesus has done in my life, even before I knew Him. He has opened my eyes to this new wonderful world, and has also begun to restore my relationship with my earthly father. I'm so grateful for that day I went to the prayer meeting, because from that point on I've been on this incredible journey of walking with Jesus. My heart has been molded, changed and fashioned to become this beautiful piece of His work. This is the journey of my heart and I wouldn't trade it for the world.

APPLICATION

What process has God taken you through in the past to bring healing to your heart?

_____

_____

_____

_____

_____

Is there a place in your heart that God is restoring right now? What is it?

_____

_____

_____

_____

_____

ACTIVATION

Put on some soaking music and ask the Father what He thinks about you. Let Him affirm you as His child and write down what He says.

_____

_____

_____

_____

_____

_____

_____

_____

_____

_____

_____

_____

_____

TRENCHES OF THE HEART

BY: MICHELLE SMITH

"This is how we know that we belong to the truth and how we set our hearts at rest in His presence: If our hearts condemn us, we know that God is greater than our hearts, and He knows everything."

1 John 3:19-20

Knowing how much God cherishes our hearts is absolutely vital to the process of growing closer to Him. As the word says, our hearts condemn us, and in those times God draws us unto Himself, assuring us that He is far greater than any condition or state of our hearts.

Living in a community that is intentionally pursuing healing of the heart and relationship can be very challenging. When I moved into this community in Shawnee, Oklahoma, and began spending time in this environment where people live with their hearts open to one another and to God, I quickly realized how closed my heart was. I desired healing in areas of my heart, but I was afraid of being vulnerable and showing any weakness. I was afraid of being completely honest when it came to any of my shortcomings or unpleasant characteristics. I would simply avoid it.

Since I was in an environment safe enough to let my walls down, I finally began dealing with the sludge that had been buried and suppressed for so long. Venturing into the trenches of my heart, in a community that intentionally pursues love, has proven the faithfulness of God to cherish and protect my heart.

"The heart of man is the treasure of the Lord and His desire is to see His people completely healed..."

Because "He is greater than our hearts, and He knows everything," He is not afraid of our sin and shortcomings. He does not run from those things that are hidden; He already knows them. Experiencing how gently God handles every matter of the heart has given me such hope for a continual process of healing and allowed me to dive into the deepest trenches of my heart.

APPLICATION

What areas of your heart have been ignored or suppressed? Where have you built walls to protect yourself?

_____

_____

_____

_____

_____

_____

_____

ACTIVATION

Ask the Holy Spirit to show you how He wants you to deal with those ignored and suppressed areas. Ask Him if you will be safe without the walls that have been protecting you. If He says yes, ask Him to break down your walls. Ask the Holy Spirit what He wants to give you in place of the walls.

_____

_____

_____

_____

_____

_____

_____

_____

_____

_____

_____

_____

_____

_____

_____

_____

_____

_____

_____

_____

_____

ALL THINGS NEW

BY: TANNON HERMAN

"Therefore, if anyone is in Christ, he is a new creation. The old has passed away; behold, the new has come."

2 Corinthians 5:17, ESV

Have you ever heard this message and still feel like the truth of being a "new creation" isn't what you're feeling or experiencing? Or maybe you believe this truth but find it difficult to consistently live out of this reality? This is exactly where I have spent the majority of my life as a believer. In fact, most people I know are still struggling to receive this truth. In many services I have attended throughout my life, there always seems to be a battle in the minister's delivery of honoring the capacity of our new nature in light of our old one. I always felt disconcerted by the lack of confidence portrayed in our ability to actually overcome sin and live righteously, but it was all I knew.

The issue in my own life was that although I had become a new creation, I was never aware I was made wholly new. I had a mental picture of myself as a man who was split down the middle being half old, half new; the old being my sin nature, the new being my nature in Christ. As I began to dive into the Scriptures for myself, I discovered throughout the gospels and letters from Paul, the truth of inherent newness portrayed confidently and without excuse. In the scripture above, Paul's "therefore" is making this truth plain and clear. This is simply how it is. You, as a believer, are totally and completely new; no gray area, no split down the middle.

"His desire is to see His people... established as sons and daughters."

In my old nature I was a slave to sin, but in my new nature I am a son of God. The entirety of the Bible points to this one thing: the redemption of man to his original intent and purpose as a son of God. Until Jesus, we had no chance in making this happen for ourselves, but God provided a way through the death of His son so we may enjoy our true design once again. Jesus' life and death drew a line in the sand of man's identity. I can no longer ride the fence; I'm in or I'm out. Because I gave my heart and life to Him, I am a new creation!

APPLICATION

How have you been viewing yourself: as a son of God or a slave to sin, or both? How has that affected your ability to overcome sin and live righteously?

_____

_____

_____

_____

_____

_____

_____

_____

ACTIVATION

Grab your Bible and highlight/underline three more scriptures emphasizing your new nature in Christ. Rewrite these passages in your own words and dialogue with the Lord about what it means to be His son.

_____

_____

_____

_____

_____

_____

_____

_____

_____

_____

_____

_____

_____

_____

_____

_____

_____

Transformational
Learning

We honor the Word of God as the foundation of truth and the catalyst for personal reformation. This experiential model of learning incorporates opportunity for the continual application of teachings coupled with group discussion and individual processing time with the Lord. The end result of this paradigm is to transform the human heart, empower a godly lifestyle, and develop mature ministry skills.

—Core Value #6—

USE IT OR LOSE IT
BY: CODY MYERS

"Do not merely listen to the Word, and so deceive yourselves. Do what it says."

James 1:22

My learning experience consisted mainly of sitting in a cubicle complete with tall blue dividers, a cabinet with cubby holes for my supplies, and a computer which was obviously developed circa 1989. I actually enjoyed school because I made good grades, but there was so much knowledge and information I lost because I didn't implement it consistently after I graduated. It wasn't until I went to the Burning Ones Discipleship School that I discovered the importance of acting on what I learn. The Apostle James describes this as doing what the Word says, not just hearing it.

One of my favorite classes in the Burning Ones was our communication course. As I practiced using the tools we were given for effective communication, I noticed my relationships becoming healthier. I was more confident about expressing how others' actions affected me, and people were more open with me as well. I loved that I got to practically apply those teachings on a daily basis. When I stepped out and did what I had been learning in the classroom, God met me in miraculous ways. He eagerly awaits the moment I take action and put His Word to the test.

"This experiential model of learning incorporates opportunity for the continual application of teachings..."

We have the incredible opportunity to be transformed by what we learn. It won't do me any good if I just take in knowledge and never act on it. The truth I find should be activated as soon as I get the chance, so that it becomes apart of me and I don't forget it. The blessing I am promised by applying what I learn not only affects me, but also those I interact with (see James 1:25). Isn't the point of the Gospel to not just hear the truth but actually live it out? I think Jesus would answer with a resounding, "Yes!"

APPLICATION

What was your learning experience like? Was it hands-on or mostly just absorbing teaching?

_____

_____

_____

_____

_____

_____

What part of living what you learn seems challenging to you? Does it empower you or scare you to think of activating truth that you find?

_____

_____

_____

_____

_____

_____

_____

ACTIVATION

Ask Holy Spirit to give you a Scripture or take one you're already meditating on and write down at least three ways you're going to implement it. It could be as practical as a service project or as inwardly focused as choosing to forgive someone. Ask for divine inspiration and grace, and then go for it!

_____

_____

_____

_____

_____

_____

_____

_____

_____

_____

PAGES IN MY HEART

BY: COLTON MCHONE

"All scripture is inspired by God and is useful to teach us what is true and to make us realize what is wrong in our lives. It corrects us when we are wrong and teaches us to do what is right."

2 Timothy 3:16, NLT

Throughout my life I have always struggled to really connect with the Bible. It seemed to either make me feel awful about myself or bore me to death. It sounded like a bunch of fictional stories taking place on another planet – it couldn't be real. I would often hear people talk about how they encountered God in a scripture or how He gave them hope through some passage, and it just didn't make sense to me. At the same time, I felt left out. It was like somehow God had forgotten to share those moments with me.

One day, my wife and a friend encouraged me to take some time to read the Bible. They assured me that God did have something for me; I just had to search and seek it out. A few weeks later, my wife and I were in a tough place, financially. Previously, we had received a large amount money, but we had unknowingly spent most of it. We had just enough to make it through the semester but felt we should pay tithe from the gift. The tithe alone was more than half of what we had left in our bank account, but we knew that God wanted us to trust Him with it.

"The end result of this paradigm is to transform the human heart, empower a godly lifestyle, and develop mature ministry skills."

Both my wife and I sat there, scared to death, worried what would become of us if we gave most of the money we had to God. Feeling desperate, I took the advice from before and opened up my Bible. I didn't know how to find things in the Bible, so I just looked in the back for keywords. I found the word *tithe* and turned to Malachi 3:10-12. The moment I read the passage I began to weep. I just knew that God was going to provide for us and that He was in control. I was also crying because I was so happy that God spoke to me through the Bible.

His Word brought a peace and understanding that I hadn't experienced before. It was in that moment I knew His Word was alive, and that it was for me, too. I know what it's like to feel bored or confused by the Bible, but that moment has changed me forever. By choosing to seek Him in His Word, I let God into my life in a new way.

APPLICATION

Are there any places in the Bible in which you feel like you are unable to connect with God? How can you change this?

_____

_____

_____

_____

_____

_____

_____

ACTIVATION

Spend some time with God in the Word. Really try and see how it's relevant to what's going on in your life. Then meditate on what God wants to do with what you've just read.

_____

_____

_____

_____

_____

_____

_____

_____

_____

_____

_____

_____

THE BIBLE IS A MAN
BY: DAVID FRITCH

"In the beginning was the Word, and the Word was with God, and the Word was God."

John 1:1

"The Bible is a man, His name is Jesus." These words radically shifted the way I approached the Word of God. The Apostle John even describes the Word as the person of Jesus (Jn. 1:1). I used to read the Bible for all the wrong reasons. I read it to prove my theological opinion, to get material for a sermon and worse yet, to earn favor with God. God began to show me that the reason He gave us the scriptures was because He wanted us to know what He was like and how He thinks and feels towards us.

This reality provoked me to read through the Bible in a relational way. So, instead of reading several chapters in one sitting, I started taking one verse at a time and talking to God about what I read. When I read something that described His nature or personality I stopped and praised Him for who He is and asked Him to show me more. Many times I would spend hours worshipping and talking to God about one single phrase.

"We honor the Word of God as the foundation of truth and the catalyst for personal reformation."

As I prayed through the Bible God revealed Himself to me and my heart came alive. One day I was reading the Lord's Prayer and began to repeat the phrase "Our Father" over and over asking God to show me what it meant that He was my Father. As I prayed my heart felt cold and my emotions were unmoved. For some reason I could not connect to God as a Father, but I continued to press into this revelation for over two weeks and finally got a breakthrough.

One day I opened my mouth to say, "Our Father," and when I did it was as if an ocean of love swept over me. These words weren't just dead letters on a page anymore. My heart came alive with the reality that God is my Dad and that He will provide and take care of me. I couldn't leave this phrase for several weeks, and every time I said it out loud the deep revelation of His heart would sweep over me again and I would begin to weep.

On that day the Word became flesh to me as I saw and felt the heart of the One I was reading about. God showed me that everything I read in the Bible was intended to lead me to an encounter with Him.

APPLICATION

Describe how you typically approach the Bible? What challenged you the most about what you read in this devotional? Why?

_____

_____

_____

_____

_____

_____

_____

ACTIVATION

Read a passage of scripture that describes what God is like (Psalm 23 is a great one). As you read this passage underline the phrases that pop out to you. Take those phrases and pray them back to God. You can praise Him, Thank Him or ask for more insight. Write down what He shows you.

_____

_____

_____

_____

_____

_____

_____

_____

_____

_____

_____

EXPERIENCE: MY GREATEST TEACHER
BY: CRISTINA HERMAN

"But the seed falling on good soil refers to someone who hears the word and understands it. This is the one who produces a crop, yielding a hundred, sixty or thirty times what was sown."

Matthew 13:23

Bill Johnson, pastor of Bethel Church in Redding, California, explains that in Eastern culture understanding means more than just mental agreement, it means knowing by experience.[3] This is the huge difference between how we as Westerners view understanding and how the Biblical Culture viewed the word understanding. This revelation makes this parable so much more powerful! Jesus is saying that in order to yield fruit in our lives we must not only hear the Word, but put it into practice through practical application and experience. Practice and experience is what actually brings real change and transformation to the human heart. Experience is meant to be our teacher that brings about the renewal of our minds.

In my own life, experiencing the supernatural has forever changed me. I grew up knowing that healing was for today. I experienced it to a small degree on and off throughout my life. But it was not until the summer of 2012 that I really understood healing. By experiencing the power of God flow through my hands and bring healing to bodies, hearts and lives I was transformed! There is something about taking the scripture and putting it into practice that changes how we think, forever. This is what Jesus wants for every believer because He knows it will bring real transformation! He wants us to take the Word of God and apply it to our lives by acting on what He says is true.

"This experiential model of learning incorporates opportunity for the continual application of teachings...The end result of this paradigm is to transform the human heart..."

---

[3] *Supernatural Power of the Transformed Mind* by Bill Johnson

On our summer mission trip, the BurnWagon, we experienced an exponential outpouring of healings and miracles. In one day alone we saw over 50 people get healed, and over the three weeks, we saw a total of 100 healings. Up to this point in my life, I had never seen that many healings. The more I experienced the supernatural, the more my mind was being renewed. I knew I was different after I came back home and continued to see healings happen on a regular basis. Yes, I still have choices to make everyday to walk in this revelation, stir it up, and continue to release Heaven to Earth. Even when I don't see results all the time, I must remind myself of what He has done in the past and that He is faithful to do it again!

APPLICATION

Think of a time that you experienced a truth from scripture. How did this bring about real change in your life?

_____

_____

_____

_____

_____

ACTIVATION

Write down 3 truths from scripture, which you believe in your mind, but have never experienced in your life. Ask the Lord to help you step out and take action on these truths. Journal about what happened to you when you actually stepped out and acted on these truths.

_____

_____

_____

_____

_____

_____

_____

_____

_____

BUT BE TRANSFORMED
BY: TANNON HERMAN

"Do not be conformed to this world, but be transformed by the renewal of your mind, that by testing you may discern what is the will of God, what is good and acceptable and perfect."

Romans 12:2, ESV

In essence, Paul is saying to the Romans, "Hey! Don't you know that God wants your mind and body just as much as your heart? Go ahead. Give Him everything. This is how you know Him." God really does want all of who we are to be transformed. Why? Because He wants His children to know His heart - what is good, acceptable (or pleasing) and perfect.

In my own life, I tried to give God my body without fully surrendering my heart and mind. I didn't realize it at the time, but I wasn't any better than the Pharisees that Jesus confronted. I thought that the devotion of my actions was real transformation, but I soon discovered that I didn't really know Him. As I approached graduating high school I became more afraid of God than ever because I didn't know what was "good and acceptable and perfect." It was in that moment of fear that I cried out to God for answers, but there were no answers.

"the Word of God... is the catalyst for personal reformation."

After I finished my first semester in college, the Holy Spirit reminded me of that unfinished conversation. He showed me that God wanted more than my outward obedience. He wanted my heart and my mind, too. Why would He want them? Because He wanted all of me to be transformed. He longed for me to know Him, and I couldn't know His heart in the midst of my fear. The shift happened as I began to read the Bible and meditate on the truth of His words. Today, I recall that conversation with Holy Spirit often as a reminder that part of my job description is to *be transformed*: continually realigned and renewed by His word so that I might know His will.

APPLICATION

Many people think of transformation as an external activity, but Paul references the mind. Why is it important for your mind to be transformed?

_____

_____

_____

_____

_____

How have you been transformed by the Word of God?

_____

_____

_____

_____

ACTIVATION

Find 3 passages of scripture that address God's plan for your life. Take a few minutes to dialogue with God about His plans for you. Write down what you experienced.

_____

_____

_____

_____

_____

_____

_____

_____

_____

_____

_____

_____

DISCOVERING THE GREATEST TREASURE
BY: MICHELLE SMITH

"I rejoice in Your word like one who discovers a great treasure."

Psalm 119:162, NLT

Before I was a Christian, I was passionately seeking answers to the truths about life, death, Heaven, God, and religion. When I was in high school I met a young man who talked about Jesus as if He was his best friend. When he said that he heard God's voice, I became particularly curious about Christianity. He was different than other Christians that I had met; his passion was contagious and he seemed to live in a different reality than anyone I had ever met before - a reality where God was real and alive. This was entirely new to me, and everything in me longed for that sense of assurance in the Divine.

My friend began sharing testimonies with me and telling me stories from the Bible. For some reason, it was hard for me to understand that these incredible things were happening in the name of God, and I had never heard of anything like them before. I thought, "If people are being raised from the dead and healed of cancer, why doesn't everyone in the world know about it?!" All of the storytelling quickly led me to action. I went to the store, just a few weeks after having these conversations, and I bought a Bible. I was hungry for truth. Part of me wanted to prove my friend wrong, but a bigger part of me wanted to believe that people really were raised from the dead and that there really is a savior for mankind.

"the Word of God is the foundation of truth..."

I dove into the Word with ravenous hunger. Every day I read more and more; I couldn't get enough of the Word. In just three months, I had read the Bible from cover to cover. God was using the truths of His Word to soften my heart. Within a month, I had a radical encounter with Jesus where I gave my heart to Him. As a believer, the joys of unlocking His Word are infinitely better because the Holy Spirit illuminates the truth. Just as the psalmist wrote, my heart comes alive at the Word of God, "like one who discovers a great treasure."

I believe that because of my foundation in His Word, God placed a deep assurance in my heart that His Word is life and truth. Just as my personal journey with the Lord began in His Word, I believe every personal breakthrough I experience will be supported by and brought to light by His Word.

APPLICATION

What experiences or encounters have you had that have proven God's word to be true? What is your favorite scripture and why?

_____

_____

_____

_____

_____

_____

_____

ACTIVATION

Meditate on Psalm 119. This chapter is the psalmist's declaration of his love for the Word of God. Choose one or two verses to journal about.

_____

_____

_____

_____

_____

_____

_____

_____

_____

_____

_____

_____

_____

_____

_____

_____

Supernatural Lifestyle

It is a way of life fueled by God's love, and rooted in the belief that man is a co-laborer with God to see Heaven invade Earth. In this divine partnership it is normal for believers to demonstrate the power of the gospel by healing the sick, receiving prophetic revelation, casting out demons and seeing the lost come to Christ. It is a naturally supernatural lifestyle.

—Core Value #7—

KEEP YOUR LOVE ON
BY: CODY MYERS

"We love because He first loved us."

1 John 4:19

For the fourteen years I've had a relationship with God, I have always wanted to see His power show up in my life. I believed healings, miracles, signs and wonders were possible, but I didn't know how to access them personally. I thought I must have colossal-sized faith in order for the supernatural to be a normal part of life. Little did I know, it wasn't just my faith that needed to grow but my capacity to love that needed stretching as well.

When I try to recall what changed my perspective on living supernaturally, my mind goes back to when I was a part of weekly outreaches. I was not very excited about ministering to people. I knew my heart was not in the right place, especially if I was considering going into full-time ministry. That was when I first started praying, "God, let me love people like You do." As I write this, I am now realizing the weight of that prayer and how it has impacted the way I live.

"It is a way of life fueled by the love of God..." By asking God to use me to distribute His love, I was asking Him to show me how much He loved me. Through spending intimate time with Him, I began to see my own value and also the value of His other children. I was becoming less concerned about doing ministry and more interested in simply loving people the way I was being loved. That was when my heart was ignited to see people healed, delivered and touched by Heaven.

I saw in the life of Jesus that it was His love, the love His Father had given Him, which moved Him to action. If I stay in my Father's love, His love stays in me and flows through me as power. I want to love people in whatever way they need it. This is what drives me to pray for the man with cancer and see him healed, or give an encouraging prophetic word to the girl working the cash register. We all need to know the glorious, powerful love He wants to lavish on us so it can flow through us at all times.

I am now experiencing just a piece of the supernatural lifestyle we were all meant for. I know there is so much more as I continue to let Father God love people through me.

APPLICATION

What has been your perception of a supernatural lifestyle? Have you viewed it as a realistic concept? Why or why not?

_____

_____

_____

_____

What are your thoughts about love being the basis of supernatural living? How would this idea change the way you live?

_____

_____

_____

_____

_____

ACTIVATION

Ask Jesus to show you any barriers that have kept you from walking in the supernatural, and let Him give you truth for lies. Write down what He tells you.

_____

_____

_____

_____

Study 1 John 4 on your own time and ask Holy Spirit to give you a new revelation of love. Write down at least four ways you will love people over the next week. Get creative with it!

1. _____
2. _____
3. _____
4. _____

A DIVINE ENCOUNTER

BY: COURTNEY YATES

> "The Spirit Himself testifies with our spirit that we are God's children. Now if we are children, then we are heirs - heirs of God and co-heirs with Christ, if indeed we share in His sufferings in order that we may also share in His glory."
>
> Romans 8: 16-17

I was sitting in a coffee house in Shawnee, Oklahoma one afternoon daydreaming with Jesus about my journey with Him and suddenly I felt His presence draw near. I felt such joy, hope, and love. I started giggling and crying to myself in the Spirit when a man passed by that seemed curious about the state I was in. I looked up to say hello and as we began to talk he told me he was depressed because he had recently become homeless and didn't know what to do. I asked him if I could pray for him and his eyes lit up as he said, "Yes, please do!"

I invited the Holy Spirit's presence to come as I prayed and I spoke life over this precious son of God. I felt the tangible presence of God fill the room and as I did he started crying. When we finished he was so full of joy and kept thanking me for praying for him. The Lord placed it on my heart to tell him that he has a pure heart. He began to cry even more and told me that he prays for himself but no one else ever asks to pray for him.

"It is a way of life fueled by God's love, and rooted in the belief that man is a co-laborer with God to see Heaven invade Earth."

This man needed an encounter with the real, fully present God. He was homeless, lost, and needed his Father to remind him that he is a son of God and that God is faithful to provide for him. God could have done this all by Himself but He wanted me to be apart of this moment with Him. This is what it means to co-labor with God as His children to to bring Heaven to Earth. These moments are the ones I live for.

APPLICATION

Has there ever been a time in your life where you can look back and see how the Lord used you to release His love into someone else's life? If so, describe it. If not, ask the Holy Spirit to reveal to you a time when you two worked together but you just didn't see it.

_____

_____

_____

_____

_____

_____

_____

_____

_____

_____

_____

_____

ACTIVATION

Spend some time with the Lord dwelling on Him, His goodness, and your journey with Him. Think about all of the great things He has done for you and through you. Praise Him, thank Him and ask Him to fill you with the fruits of the Spirit. Then take that fuel you received out of your place of intimacy with Him and go look for someone who needs an encounter with the Father. You have the presence of God in you, now go release it!

_____

_____

_____

_____

_____

_____

_____

_____

_____

TACO SHOP TRANSFORMATION
BY: CRISTINA HERMAN

"Go into all the world and preach the gospel to all creation... And these signs will accompany those who believe; In My name they will drive out demons, they will speak in new tongues...they will place their hands on sick people and they will get well."

Mark 16:15, 17-18

Last summer we were in Los Fresnos, Texas on a summer mission trip across the United States called the Burn Wagon. We had just finished praying over the pastors in the area and went to eat lunch. As we were eating, the owners of the restaurant noticed we weren't locals and asked why we were in town. The pastors told them we were here to pray for people, so the owners asked if we could pray for them and their business. As we began to pray, the presence of God filled the room as our team spoke the heart of God and destiny over each worker's lives. My husband suddenly got a pain in his chest and knew it was a word of knowledge for a heart condition. We prayed for the man who had it and believed he was instantly healed. After prophesying over them, we felt the urge to simply ask them if they had ever heard the story of Jesus. They had never heard, but after receiving prophecy and healing they were eager to hear about this man who had touched their lives. Upon hearing the gospel, all three of them gave their lives to Jesus right there in the middle of a taco shop.

"In this divine partnership it is normal for believers to demonstrate the power of the gospel by healing the sick, receiving prophetic revelation, casting out demons and seeing the lost come to Christ."

We were overjoyed at how simple it was for them to come to Christ. Our team was very familiar with prophesying over people and praying for the sick, but we had somehow forgotten that the point of demonstrating the Kingdom is to introduce the King to His kids. It was so easy for them to receive Jesus, because the power of the gospel had demonstrated His love for them and they wanted to know this God we had shown them. This is why we need to walk in the power of God, to demonstrate the love of Jesus so unbelievers can know Him. This is meant for every believer, that no matter where we are, whether eating tacos or at Walmart, we can demonstrate His Kingdom. This is what it means to be naturally supernatural.

APPLICATION

Do you feel like you demonstrate the power of the gospel on a regular basis? Why or why not?

_____

_____

_____

_____

_____

_____

ACTIVATION

Step out and pray for at least one person every day this week as you are going about your everyday life. Every morning, ask the Lord to give you words of knowledge or clues about the person you are supposed to pray for. Then as you are out in public, ask the Lord to show you who those clues are for. Look for the clues and ask the person God shows you if you can pray for them. If it is for healing, ask them how they feel on a scale from 1-10 before and then again after you pray for them. Have them test it out if possible. Journal about your experience.

_____

_____

_____

_____

_____

_____

_____

_____

_____

_____

_____

_____

HEAVEN ON EARTH

BY: JOSHUA SWARNY

"So He said to them, 'When you pray, say: Our Father in Heaven, hallowed be Your name. Your kingdom come. Your will be done on earth as it is in Heaven.'"

Luke 11:2, NKJV

In the above passage, Jesus is responding to His disciples' question about how to pray. This prayer establishes how important it is to know God as Father. We are meant to live in relationship with Him. He is a Father burning with love for His children. If God does everything out of love, then we should do the same.

This prayer also addresses our role as sons to co-labor with the Father. Jesus told us to pray, "Your kingdom come. Your will be done on earth as it is in Heaven." He wants us to release Heaven on Earth in partnership with Him, a kingdom that is full of life and love. Because God has shown His extravagant love toward me, I desire for others to encounter that same love.

Jesus said the kingdom of Heaven is at hand (see Matt. 3:2). Jesus is telling us that right now we have access to this kingdom of life. I see so many people who *"It is a way of life fueled by God's love, and rooted in the belief that man is a co-laborer with God to see Heaven invade Earth."* do not know the reality of life through Jesus. They seem well acquainted with sickness, disease, depression and poverty, and less acquainted with love and freedom.

One day as I was looking for a movie in a video store I saw a girl with a knee brace on. I approached her and asked if I could pray for her. She allowed me to pray and even expressed that her college roommate believes in supernatural healing. The pain was the same as before I prayed for her, but she assured me it was okay. She tried to comfort me by saying, "God afflicts us so that we can be a testimony of praising Him even through our pain." Her response upset me deeply. I would hope she could praise the Lord through her pain, but I cannot convince myself that God has lovingly afflicted her with pain. I gently encouraged her that God wants us to be testimonies of His life and power.

God is not punishing people with sickness, emotional crises, poverty or demonic spirits. Why would He give His life for us and then torture us? God is wanting and waiting for someone to partner with His will to release His kingdom of love on the earth.

I am practicing partnering with God by releasing Heaven to invade Earth. Everyone I pray for does not get healed. But with every prayer I pray, I am agreeing with God's will that each person would come to know the Father's love. Living a supernatural lifestyle starts with love. Love for God and then love for people. By releasing His love, His kingdom is established and I will begin to see more people freed from their afflictions.

APPLICATION

How has your life exemplified love? Has it been accompanied with healing power? Explain.

_____

_____

_____

_____

ACTIVATION

Dream and journal about what it would look like for God's kingdom of love to come to Earth.

_____

_____

_____

_____

_____

_____

Write down one way you can bring God's kingdom of love to the earth today and then do it!

_____

_____

_____

_____

LOVE IS POWER

BY: TANNON HERMAN

"Jesus went through all the towns and villages, teaching in their synagogues, preaching the good news of the kingdom and healing every disease and sickness. When He saw the crowds, He had compassion on them, because they were harassed and helpless, like sheep without a shepherd."

Matthew 9:35-36

Formerly, I thought the power of Jesus was His Divinity He used in order to prove His message. I thought that if He encountered someone of power, He would use His power to reveal His omnipotence. Jesus, in my head, could never be wholly man - after all, I had never heard of another man with that kind of power. What was it about Jesus that made Him so powerful? How is it possible that He could heal multitudes of people in a moment?

It all clicked for me one day when I began focusing on Jesus' emotions as He demonstrated the gospel through power. In the passage above, I noticed that Jesus' need to demonstrate His authority wasn't the reason He would heal people - it was His compassion. Jesus didn't have to wait on the Lord to give Him direction in these moments; He knew His Father's heart. Jesus understood that peoples' lives and bodies weren't healed simply by some power from another world, but by the love of the Father. I believe that when Jesus aligned Himself to love people the way that His Father loved them, that is when the miraculous power manifested.

"It is a way of life fueled by God's love..."

In my own life, I have prayed for hundreds of people. More often than not, the people left those encounters without the very thing I was praying for. At that point in my life I prayed for people because that is what I was supposed to do. Jesus prayed for the sick so I will pray for the sick. But I was missing the key element that led Jesus to pray for people - love. When I recognized my prayers and efforts were lacking love, I learned to lean on the Father's heart to teach me, as He did Jesus, to love people with His heart of compassion.

Since that moment of revelation, I still don't see everyone get healed instantaneously, but I am astounded at how many more people are encountering the healing power of His love. My prayer is no longer, "God, I want power to heal people like Jesus." My desire now is to love people radically and wholeheartedly like my Daddy does. To act like Jesus is one thing; to love like Him is another thing entirely.

APPLICATION

What has it meant to you to be "powerful" as a believer?

_____

_____

_____

_____

_____

_____

_____

ACTIVATION

Take a moment to pray and ask God to show you how He feels about people. Afterwards, ask the Lord to show you how to love people like He does. Write what He tells you in your journal, and then share the love with others!

_____

_____

_____

_____

_____

_____

_____

_____

_____

_____

_____

_____

NATURALLY SUPERNATURAL
BY: DAVID FRITCH

"As you go, preach this message: 'The kingdom of Heaven is near.' Heal the sick, raise the dead, cleanse those who have leprosy, drive out demons."

Matthew 10:7-8a

Every summer we take teams of young people across the United States on a mission trip called the BurnWagon. The mission of the BurnWagon is two-fold: gather the church to worship and pray for revival and minister the gospel in the streets with signs and wonders following. Every year God does incredible things, but in the summer of 2012 God took our ministry to a whole new level. We saw one hundred and fifty instant healings on the streets and 35 people give their lives to Jesus.

The West Coast team was in Las Vegas ministering on the main strip every night; singing, preaching and praying for the sick with very little results. One night we decided to let the team have a break, so we went to get some frozen yogurt. As we entered the shopping area I began to feel a sharp pain in my back and felt like God was telling me that someone with back pain needed healing.

Right after I heard God speak to me four people, wearing black, covered in tattoos and piercings, passed by. Without even thinking I blurted out, "Hey do any of you *"In this divine partnership it is normal for believers to demonstrate the power of the gospel by healing the sick..."* have back pain?" One of the men spoke up and told us he had had fourteen surgeries on his back and that he was in constant pain. We prayed a simple fifteen-second prayer and then asked him to check himself for pain. He began to bend over and move from side to side, and then with a surprised look on his face told us all the pain was gone! We had a chance to share the love of Jesus with him and pray for his walk with the Lord to be strengthened.

I love that this miracle didn't happen on any of our planned outreaches but as we were relaxing and having and fun. I believe God wants to heal and save people through us, not just at events but as a lifestyle. All we have to do is be aware of His presence and look for opportunities each day. Very often I will ask the Lord to give me words of knowledge of who I'm supposed to pray for before I go to the grocery store. My little list of physical symptoms I write down causes me to be aware of the people around me and to look for opportunities to pray for them. Recently, on my way to Walmart, God told me that I would minister to someone with knee pain. As I was shopping I was looking for people with canes, braces or in motorized scooters. In the check-out lane, I saw a man in a scooter and asked him what the problem was. It turns out he had severe arthritis in the (you guessed it) knees. I prayed for him and God instantly took away the pain.

Moving in the supernatural should be the most natural part of our lives as believers in Jesus. If you are hungry to be used by God, just begin to ask for opportunities and begin to pray for people everywhere you go. Don't be afraid to chase down people in scooters or take a risk to approach total strangers. As you take a risk God will show up.

APPLICATION

What about this devotional has challenged you to walk in the supernatural? What are you going to do about it?

_____

_____

_____

_____

ACTIVATION

Take a few minutes and ask God to show you three physical problems people need healing for. Then head off to the grocery store or the mall. Look for people with those needs or ask God to show you who the people are. When you find them tell them you would like to pray that God would heal them. Ask them to tell you what their pain level is on a scale of 1-10. Then pray a very short prayer, no longer than 15 seconds, and ask them to check the pain level. If all the pain doesn't go away then ask if you can pray one more time. If they get healed then introduce them to their Healer, Jesus!

UNUSUAL AND UNEXPECTED
BY: MICHELLE SMITH

"God gave Paul the power to perform unusual miracles."

Acts 19:11, NLT

One of my favorite things about God is how extravagant and sometimes unexpected His miracles are. What is ordinary to Him is extraordinary to me, even unfathomable sometimes. Just like Paul and the early church, God still uses us to perform unusual miracles on the earth today.

I was ministering in Boise, Idaho with a team from Bethel Church. After a teaching about healings, a few of us went to the front to minister. We shared what we felt God was doing in that place. One by one, my teammates called out cancer, knee pain, and back injuries. Then it was my turn. The only picture I had in my mind was a scar. I said, "I believe God wants to heal scars today." The next person in line shared what they were sensing, and we offered prayer to anyone who wanted it.

"In this divine partnership it is normal for believers to demonstrate the power of the gospel"

About an hour after the meeting, a gentleman came up to me with a look of shock on his face. He held out his arm as if he was going to show me something, and began telling me a story. When he was a child, he had an accident which left a long scar from his wrist up along his forearm. As he was telling me this, with wide eyes, he finished with, "Look!" His arm was perfect and unscarred. God had removed the scar that he had had for decades, just to show this man how much He loved him and that He is a supernatural God who still performs miracles today.

Experiencing God supernaturally heal a man's scar gave me faith for other unusual miracles. It was evidence for me that God cares not only about things that are necessary and urgent, but He cares about every detail of our lives. He is the God who knows how many hairs are on our heads, and for Him, erasing a scar is just plain fun!

APPLICATION

How have you experienced or been impacted by the supernatural miracles of God? What would you like to see God do through you?

_____
_____
_____
_____
_____
_____
_____
_____
_____
_____
_____
_____
_____
_____

ACTIVATION

Ask God how He wants to display His miraculous powers today. Ask for specific words of knowledge or clues concerning people He wants you to minister to.

_____
_____
_____
_____
_____
_____
_____
_____
_____
_____
_____
_____
_____
_____
_____

Global Revival

The life of Christ empowers the Church to violently advance His Kingdom into all nations of the earth. We believe that the nations are our inheritance and global transformation is achieved through partnership with God in night and day prayer and worship, radical love for humanity and powerful demonstrations of the gospel. We are contending for the church world-wide to be fully awakened to the love of God and to have faith for entire cities to be transformed.

—Core Value #8—

YOU ARE THE ANSWER TO YOUR PRAYERS
BY: DAVID FRITCH

> "Ask of Me and I will surely give the nations as your inheritance"
>
> Psalm 2:8a. NASB

Several years ago I led a weekly prayer meeting for the Middle East with the Burning Ones Discipleship School students. When I learned that ancient Nineveh is now the modern Iraqi city of Mosul, my heart was provoked to contend for an outpouring of the Spirit there. I began praying, "God if you could transform a pagan city like Nineveh in a single day then you could surely do it again." As I was crying out to God a violent spirit of prayer came on me, and I began to groan and pray in tongues.

I was slightly embarrassed that I was making so many strange noises and screaming at the top of my lungs, but soon all my self-consciousness left as I was caught up in a heavenly battle for the city of Mosul. It was as if God took over my whole body and prayed through me. After about an hour of this, the Spirit lifted from me and when I looked around the room everyone was staring at me in amazement. I just shrugged

"Global transformation is achieved through partnership with God in night and day prayer and worship..."

my shoulders and said, "I wonder what that was all about?" God didn't show me what I was praying for that day, but I would soon find out that God used our little prayer team to shift the destiny of Iraq.

The next day I was online searching for newspaper articles about the city of Mosul, and what I discovered absolutely blew my mind. I read a report that on the very day we prayed for Mosul they busted 54 Al Qaeda terrorists and prevented two car bombs from going off. The article said this was the last Al Qaeda stronghold in Mosul which they had been pursuing for months!

Needless to say my passion to see the nation of Iraq come to Jesus exploded. My prayers became more focused and fierce for an outpouring in this nation. I want to warn you that when you begin to pray for something, God will often make you the answer to your own prayers. One year later God sent me to Iraq, with an organization called the Burn 24-7, to plant a night and day worship and prayer ministry. The results of that trip were staggering as it led to dozens of people getting saved and healed.

Prayer is the starting place for seeing global revival. God implores of us, "Ask of me and I will surely give you the nations as your inheritance" (Ps. 2:8). The founder of the Methodist Church, John Wesley, said, "God never does anything in the earth except through believing prayer." If this is true then we have the incredible honor and mandate to partner with God, through prayer, to reach the ends of the earth.

APPLICATION

What could God do in your city, on your campus or at your church if you rallied people to pray? Take a minute to write out your thoughts.

_____

_____

_____

_____

_____

_____

_____

ACTIVATION

Ask the Lord to show you what nation He wants you to start praying for. Take some time to lift that country before the Lord and write down anything He shows you. Keep a journal as you pray for this over the next few weeks.

_____

_____

_____

_____

_____

_____

_____

_____

STIRRING UP THE CITIES

BY: CODY MYERS

"When Jesus entered Jerusalem, the whole city was stirred and asked, 'Who is this?'"

Matthew 21:10

Jesus entered the city of Jerusalem while the crowds shouted, "Hosanna!" He was the King of Kings and Lord of Lords, but He arrived on a donkey. He didn't storm in on a white steed or with an army of servants tending to His every whim. Yet, His arrival caused such a commotion, the entire city wanted to know what was going on.

I have been on several mission trips to cities in the United States where children of God truly believed they could influence their city and see it transformed. They knew this was the commission the Lord had given them. One of those groups was Youth with a Mission in Las Vegas. They are zealous believers living and ministering in the heart of the most dangerous places in the city. They do not let negative opinions or religious persecution stop them from spreading the message of God's love through their words, worship, and actions. As they have pressed through physical and spiritual hindrances, their light has demanded attention and they have begun to stir the curiosity of the people in the city.

"We are contending for the church worldwide...to have faith for entire cities to be transformed."

It encourages me to partner with such passionate disciples as it inspires me to contend for my own city. I can pray for transformation, but why not be willing to be the answer to my own prayer? That's what I see Jesus doing in the gospels. He was a teacher who led by example. He showed me how to partner with my Father to bring about a reformation. The Spirit of God inside of me is my revival mentor, and He is equipping me to shift the culture I live in.

My continual prayer is that I will never perform out of my own strength, but that I will stay close to my Father's heart and do what I see Him doing. This attitude takes the pressure and intimidation out of contending for revival. I want a fire of love to burn so wildly in me that it sets my community on fire and causes a stir in the hearts of the people around me.

How would I live my life if I truly believed that the destiny of my city is in my hands? History is just waiting to be written by one crazy enough to pick up a pen and write it.

APPLICATION

Does the idea of city transformation excite you or intimidate you? If so, in what ways?

_____

_____

_____

_____

Think over your walk with Christ and ask yourself: Does the way I live make people ask questions about whom and what I know? Why or why not?

_____

_____

_____

_____

ACTIVATION

Take some time to dream and write about what you would do in your city if you had total authority. If you are really up for the challenge, do this same activity on a national scale, and then a global scale.

_____

_____

_____

Ask the Lord which dream you can pick to put into action right now. Write down goals and practical steps you will take in partnering with Him to see it come to pass.

_____

_____

_____

_____

_____

FROM DEATH INTO LIFE
BY: MICHELLE SMITH

"As you go, preach this message: 'The kingdom of Heaven is near.' Heal the sick, raise the dead, cleanse those who have leprosy, drive out demons. Freely you have received, freely give."

Matthew 10:7-8

When I was 19 years-old I went on my first mission trip to the Baja California peninsula in Mexico with Bethel Church out of Redding, California. We spent a week teaching about the supernatural power of God and also sharing the Gospel in the community through house visits, drama productions, outreaches, and open-air worship services.

At the end of the week, one of my teammates taught about God's power to raise people from the dead. He shared testimonies and the entire church broke out in energetic worship. Near the end of the evening, a woman ran frantically into the room with tears running down her face. She was hysterical and clearly wanted our attention.

"We believe that the nations are our inheritance and global transformation is achieved through... powerful demonstrations of the gospel."

Her story came spilling out, and our translator did his best to keep up. She had been in the meeting earlier that night and heard the testimonies of people being raised from the dead. In the middle of the meeting, her daughter showed up in a distraught state and they left immediately. She ran home to find her husband dead on the floor of her home. He had a heart attack and quit breathing about twenty minutes before she arrived. When the woman showed up, full of faith and having only one hope, she laid hands on her husband and prayed a simple prayer of desperation, "God, raise my husband from the dead."

After about one minute of praying and crying out to God, her husband's lungs were filled with air and he began choking. He came back to life! God had miraculously raised him from the dead. As her story was shared with the congregation, everyone fell to their knees weeping and worshiping God. A sense of awe and power filled the room in a way that I have yet to experience again.

That day I experienced how God supernaturally releases the power of His Gospel in the nations. Whether at home or in a foreign land, our commission is the same: to release His kingdom. The powerful exploits I saw on that trip in Mexico awakened a hunger in me to see God's name exalted and praised in the nations. No people group, no race, no ethnicity, and no nation are left out of God's plan for revival. He is worthy of all of our praise and adoration. There is truly no God like our God.

APPLICATION

How does the power of the Gospel help us inherit the nations?

_____

_____

_____

_____

_____

_____

ACTIVATION

Spend some time worshiping God and meditating on how holy and worthy He is. Next, envision what global revival could look like. Ask God to speak to you and give you visions of a world transformed by His Gospel. Share what God has shown you with friends. Let your dreams and visions encourage one another.

_____

_____

_____

_____

_____

_____

_____

_____

_____

HEAVEN IN ME

BY: COLTON MCHONE

"I saught the Lord, and He answered me; He delivered me from all my fears."

Psalm 54:4

The summer before I proposed to my wife we spent the summer leading worship in Jerusalem. We felt excited about this incredible opportunity to lead worship for 25 hours a week in the Holy land but we also felt anxious because we had not led worship in over a year. Even though we were insecure about our abilities we went knowing God was leading us into a once-in-a-lifetime experience.

On the day we arrived in Israel I was asked to lead worship the very next night. I nervously complied not wanting to deny the very reason I came and to ignore the call on my life to lead worship. I thought about it the whole next day until the service started at 7:00 pm. I had my songs picked out and on the outside I was ready, but on the inside I was terrified.

However, when the service began and I strummed the first chord on the guitar I immediately felt as if I were right back at home. The power of God came over me, and I began screaming my heart out. I cried out to God for the nation of Israel, for my heart, the hearts of the people and for His heart. It was like all of this worship for Jesus had been pent up inside of me, and it all got released in a one-hour set. For years people have encouraged me that I was made to lead worship, but it wasn't until this moment that I saw it in myself.

"We believe... global transformation is achieved through partnership with God in night and day prayer and worship..."

God taught me an important lesson that in my weakness He will show up with supernatural power and minister through me. That night many people were changed and impacted by the release of the Holy Spirit in worship. A few weeks later, while still in Jerusalem, I had a supernatural encounter that changed my life forever.

During worship, I suddenly felt darkness surround me. I felt overwhelmed and tormented. I didn't know what to do; I had never felt anything so terrible, and all I wanted to do was get rid of it. Not knowing of anything else to do, I went to the pastor of the church and told her what was going on. She stood up and stopped the service and had everyone start praying for me.

As they laid their hands on me and prayed, I felt a surge of power hit me. Heaven invaded my being. The presence of God came into the room. The next thing I knew, I was laying on the ground screaming. I was so scared but I did the only thing that I knew to do in that moment: I cried out the name of Jesus. He came and the darkness could not stay. I could feel the battle going on over me in the supernatural realm. Then I felt His strength come upon me. It felt like I had all of Heaven backing me and I could not lose the battle.

So I stood up and started punching my fist in the air. For some reason it just felt like the natural thing to do. Each time I punched the air, I felt more freedom coming. In that moment my spirit woke up in a way that changed my life forever. Now my spirit feels more sensitive to everything around me. God gave me this gift to break through spiritual atmospheres, so that His kingdom can continue to invade the earth.

As I trusted the power of God to help me in my fear and weakness God not only used me to bless others, but He also set me free in a way that is still impacting lives around me.

APPLICATION

How have you seen Heaven invade Earth in your own life?

_____

_____

_____

_____

_____

_____

ACTIVATION

Find a quiet place and invite Heaven to come down. If you need freedom or healing then ask. Whatever you need you can find in His presence.

THE GOSPEL DOESN'T JUST HAPPEN
BY: TANNON HERMAN

> "From the days of John the Baptist until now, the kingdom of Heaven has been forcefully advancing, and forceful men lay hold of it."
>
> Matthew 11:12

Have you ever been told that people will experience change by simply being around you? I can't tell you how many times I have been disappointed by that statement turning out to be false. I am probably not alone in saying people don't just suddenly have revelations of their need for a Savior when I walk into the room. Of course, as believers we do carry an atmosphere of Heaven with us, but carrying Heaven is an intentional agreement. Jesus didn't haphazardly share and demonstrate the gospel. Just as He says in Matthew, "the kingdom of Heaven has been *forcefully* advancing."

My own past reflects somewhat of a passive approach to expanding the borders of the kingdom. I would sit around and wait for a convenient moment to tell someone about Jesus; moreover, I was fearful about hurting someone further than they already were by offering the story of Jesus without results. If someone were to hear the story of redemption from me they must have been desperately trying

"The life of Christ empowers the Church to violently advance His Kingdom into all nations of the earth."

to get it out of me. But why? I guess I kind of figured their revelation and encounter would just... happen. Maybe they'll just wake up one day and *POOF!* Jesus would be standing right in front of them with arms wide open. That's how it happens, right?

Wrong! The gospel is more than just a coincidental experience; it is strategic warfare for the believer. Many people use the verse "but the kindness of the Lord leads to repentance" (Romans 2:4) as a way to relieve themselves from the responsibility of displaying the gospel, but even showing kindness is active. In my life experience, people have encountered the love, power and kindness of the gospel when I took it out of my box of passivity and portrayed it as loudly and brilliantly as I could. Whether it was chasing down a limping man at Walmart or singing praises at the top of my lungs in downtown Jerusalem, I was actively, forcefully advancing the kingdom. Jesus made an invitation to his followers to do something with their faith. Don't just play with it and put it back in the closet when it's time to leave the house - take it with you!

You have been given keys to a kingdom of unlimited power and resource. What are you doing with them?

APPLICATION

Has your life reflected an active or passive gospel message? Why?

_____

_____

_____

_____

What could you do to become more forceful with the kingdom?

_____

_____

_____

_____

ACTIVATION

Think of 5 ways that you can intentionally advance the kingdom today. Write them down and review your list at the end of the day. Make it a habit to live with kingdom strategy everyday.

1. _____

2. _____

3. _____

4. _____

5. _____

TO THOSE WHO HAVE NEVER HEARD
BY: CRISTINA HERMAN

> "How, then, can they call on the one they have not believed in? And how can they believe in the one of whom they have not heard? And how can they hear without someone preaching to them? And how can anyone preach unless they are sent? As it is written, 'How beautiful are the feet of those who bring good news!'"
>
> Romans 10:14-15

It was a beautiful spring Sunday afternoon and we were with our team sitting out by the Mediterranean Sea in Antalya, Turkey. It was not just any Sunday, but Easter Sunday, and we were in an Islamic nation where people had never heard the gospel. During the enitre time in Turkey we were confronted with an antichrist spirit that was trying to silence us. An antichrist spirit is a spirit that is completely against the revelation and demonstration of Christ. This spirit was telling us, "You can't really preach the gospel here, and if you do, no one will receive you and you could get into trouble. Simply preaching the gospel has not worked in the past. You must show them the gospel through your friendship." This mindset, although at first appears to be culturally sensitive, was actually the antichrist spirit at work (see 1 John 4:3). It wanted to silence our team from preaching and demonstrating the gospel with power to a people who have no knowledge and no other way of knowing Christ.

"We believe that the nations are our inheritance and global transformation is achieved through partnership with God in night and day prayer and worship, radical love for humanity and powerful demonstrations of the gospel."

As I sat in the park that day for our last outreach, I thought this could be the only time these people ever hear the gospel. This could be their only chance. That day our team was bolder than ever before and we were able to share the gospel with over twenty people. One of the conversations I had was with a young girl in her twenties. She was tired of the strict rules and regulations of Islam, but still considered herself a Muslim. She was empty and looking for anything to fill her life and heart. She had turned to alcohol, sex and relationships to fill this void, but was left unsatisfied. We were able to share the love of Jesus with her and she was so close to giving her life to Him. We challenged her to ask Jesus to reveal himself to her when she went home that day. She said she would. Who knows what happened to her that night after she went home? This is just one story of the many seeds we planted that day. It felt so good to be able to tell people the good news of Jesus Christ.

I believe what we did that day was the beginning of a breakthrough in Turkey. We challenged the antichrist spirit and dared to believe the gospel of Jesus Christ carries power to break the hardest of hearts. The harvest is ripe, but the laborers are few. Who will go to the darkest nations of the earth and tell the gospel to those who have never heard? Who will dare to believe that His word is enough to change hearts and lives? Who will risk all for the sake of His Name? There is power in the name of Jesus.

APPLICATION

Have you ever shared the gospel with someone who has never heard? If no, why not?

_____

_____

_____

_____

In what ways do you face the anti-Christ spirit here in the U.S.A when sharing the gospel?

_____

_____

_____

_____

ACTIVATION

Take time to simply preach the gospel. Ask someone this week if they have ever heard the gospel? Continue to ask, until you are able to share with someone   who   has   never   heard.

What is the Burning Ones Mission Base?

The Burning Ones Mission Base is a community of believers committed to prioritizing the presence of God as the center of life, living in authentic relationship and equipping believers to know God intimately, to walk in their identity in Christ, and to ignite revival and transformation in cities and nations through worship, prayer and supernatural evangelism. The Burning Ones Mission Base is located in Shawnee, OK and has multiple ministries including the Prayer Furnace, Burning Ones Discipleship School, Burn Wagon, International Mission, Convergence and Overflow.

Our dream is to *build and establish apostolic communities* that pursue the presence of God above all else and seek to establish the culture of Heaven on earth. These covenant families have their hope set on Heaven and are burning with zeal to transform the city they are planted in. These communities are radically committed to genuine, intentional relationships and seek to create a safe place for people to be healed and restored. It is a culture where there is freedom to be yourself, live from the heart and fulfill the work of the Lord.

Our vision is to serve as a *24-7 prayer center* that contends for the local church to be fully awakened, growing by conversions and impacting every sphere of society. Our desire is to be bridge builders between local churches and to serve as catalysts to heal the strife, misunderstanding and wounds in the Body. What would it look like if God began to answer the cries of a unified bride contending for breakthrough twenty-four hours a day?

This is a *creative community* where there is a heavenly demand on stirring and activating the dreams of the heart. We believe the fruits of a company of awakened dreamers will burst forth to shift the destiny of entire cities and nations.

This is a *supernatural environment* where every believer is equipped to hear God's voice and to release the power of the kingdom of God through signs and wonders. Our aim is to represent the culture of Heaven to our city by demonstrating both the love and power of God. We are contending for a culture where it is natural to be supernatural. We believe that the church will arise and release prophetic wisdom and supernatural power in order to bring transformation into every sphere of society.

Our dream is to see *city transformation* through the love and power of the gospel. Our hope is in the goodness and power of God to overthrow poverty, see drug trafficking ended, broken families restored and local churches living in perpetual revival, growing exponentially. Is it possible that crime statistics could be lowered every year as a result of what God is doing through the awakened church? What would it look like for the prophetic ministry to be consulted by mayors, businessmen, and government agencies? Could it be that cures for cancer are discovered in our town? Could it be that disease and sickness is completely eradicated?

The Mission Base seeks to be a *servant to the city* and to display the love of God through generous acts of kindness. What would it look like to have believers volunteer in every segment of our city? Can you imagine an army of believers who love and serve their city by restoring neighborhoods, cleaning up parks, and building homes for the homeless?

Our mandate is to be a *sending center* where people can spend seasons of their lives to get equipped, trained, restored and sent out with zeal to fulfill their God-given dreams. Our vision is to send out laborers to plant kingdom communities all over the globe that pursue the presence of God above all else, live in covenant community and practice a radical lifestyle of hope for the supernatural transformation of cities and nations.

Introduction to the Authors

DAVID FRITCH

David Fritch has spent his life serving the Lord in many capacities such as missionary, youth pastor, teacher, worship leader and pastor. However, most recently he has found his identity in and his greatest pleasure in pursuing the heart of God! Founder and Director of the Burning Ones Mission Base, David has been given the opportunity to express all the different facets of his calling: intercession, worship, mission, and discipleship. David's vision is to raise up an army of worshipers, and intercessors who are rooted and grounded in the word of God, whose character has been forged in the fire of authentic community and who burn with a passion for igniting the darkest regions of the world with the presence of God! David's heart is to see a generation released into their destiny of preparing the way for the coming King!

TANNON AND CRISTINA HERMAN

Tannon and Cristina Herman serve as the Directors of the Burning Ones Discipleship School and Burn Wagon. Both graduates of the Discipleship School in 2009, they have continued to serve with the ministry for 4 years. Tannon and Cristina actively participate in the Burning Ones Prayer Furnace and lead worship. Tannon is an amazing worship leader, with over 10 years of experience and an anointing for corporate worship. Cristina is a psalmist carrying an anointing for prophetic worship and inner-healing. They have helped to pioneer "covenant community" in the Burning Ones ministry and are passionate about equipping believers for authentic relationship with others. Both Tannon and Cristina have a heart for the nations and are very passionate about activating the body of Christ to walk in the supernatural power of the gospel. Together they have visited over 20 nations with the Gospel and continue to lead teams every year across the globe.

COURTNEY YATES

Courtney Yates is a graduate of the Burning Ones Discipleship School and Leadership Development Community of 2012. She is a passionate lover of Jesus with a heart to carry prophetic worship and supernatural evangelism to the ends of the earth. Courtney has a heart to see women set free and empowered to walk in their identity in Christ. She currently serves as the youth worship leader at a local church and is actively involved in the Prayer Furnace and Burning Ones Mission Base community.

CODY MYERS

Cody Myers is a graduate of the Burning Ones Discipleship School and Leadership Development Community of 2012. She is a dynamic worship leader with an anointing to shift atmospheres through her worship. Cody has a heart to disciple young people and wants to eventually plant a Burning Ones Discipleship School in India. She currently serves the Burning Ones Mission Base and is actively involved in the Prayer Furnace in leading worship. In January, Cody will continue preparing for her dream through serving as a Burning Ones Intern in our next Burning Ones Discipleship School.

JOSHUA SWARNY

Joshua Swarny is a Leadership Development Community graduate of 2012. He is an extremely talented drummer with an anointing to bring freedom through his worship. Joshua has a huge heart to see unity manifest in the body of Christ. He is an amazing photographer and videographer, and is currently pursuing his dream to start a photography business. Joshua is actively involved in the Burning Ones Mission Base Community, leading worship and sets at the Prayer Furnace. Joshua also is planning to return as an intern to help with Burning Ones Discipleship School in the coming year.

MICHELLE SMITH

Michelle Smith is a Leadership Development Community graduate of 2012. She recently moved to join our community all the way from Waterville, Maine. Michelle is a very passionate and fun-loving person and brings so much joy to everyone she encounters! She has a heart for worship, creativity and the nations. Michelle also has a huge dream to see revival and transformation come to the college campuses of America. Michelle is currently working at St. Gregory's University and is an active part of the Burning Ones Mission Base Community leading worship.

COLTON MCHONE

Colton McHone is a graduate of the Burning Ones Discipleship School of 2010 and Leadership Development Community of 2012. He has a heart of worship and carries a unique sound to bring healing and wholeness to the brokenness of our generation. Colton has a dream to transform this generation through his music and is currently working on his first album. He is actively involved in the Burning Ones Mission Base Community. Colton is currently studying Graphic Design at Full Sail University and is married to his beautiful wife, Kim, who is studying Law at OU.

For more information:

Burning Ones Mission Base
230 N Broadway Ave
Shawnee, OK 74801

www.burningones.com

What is the Burning Ones Discipleship School?

...cultivate intimacy with God as your highest priority...

...get equipped for supernatural outreach...

...RESTORE YOUR GOD-GIVEN IDENTITY...

...travel across the USA lighting revival fires...

...discover your dreams, gifts & calling...

...train in an atmosphere of night & day worship/prayer...

...TAKE THE GOSPEL TO THE NATIONS...

...develop deep, life-changing relationships...

For more information:

www.burningones.com/training

e-mail: contact@burningones.com

BURNWAGON

The BurnWagon is a **mission trip** across the United States that carries the fire of **His presence** through worship, intercession and supernatural evangelism. Teams join with local believers to **contend for revival** and **activate** the body of Christ to reach the lost with the power of the Gospel.

BurnWagon teams consist of musicians, dancers, artists, intercessors, revivalists and all others who have a heart to see America return to her first love and the Church rise as the victorious Bride of Christ.

For more information:
www.burnwagon.com // contact@burnwagon.com